LABYRINTH OF WIND

LABYRINTH OF WIND

Poems and Collages

A collaboration by
Terriann Walling and Clive Knights

Labyrinth of Wind

ISBN 978-0-9959845-8-5

Cover art: Daedalus by Clive Knights

First printing edition 2024

Terriann Walling, poet
@walling.terriann
www.terriannwalling.com

Clive Knights, collagist
@knightsclive
www.cliveknights.com

This book is dedicated to the artists' residency at Chateau d'Orquevaux in France, and to all our co-residents from June 30th to July 14th, 2022.

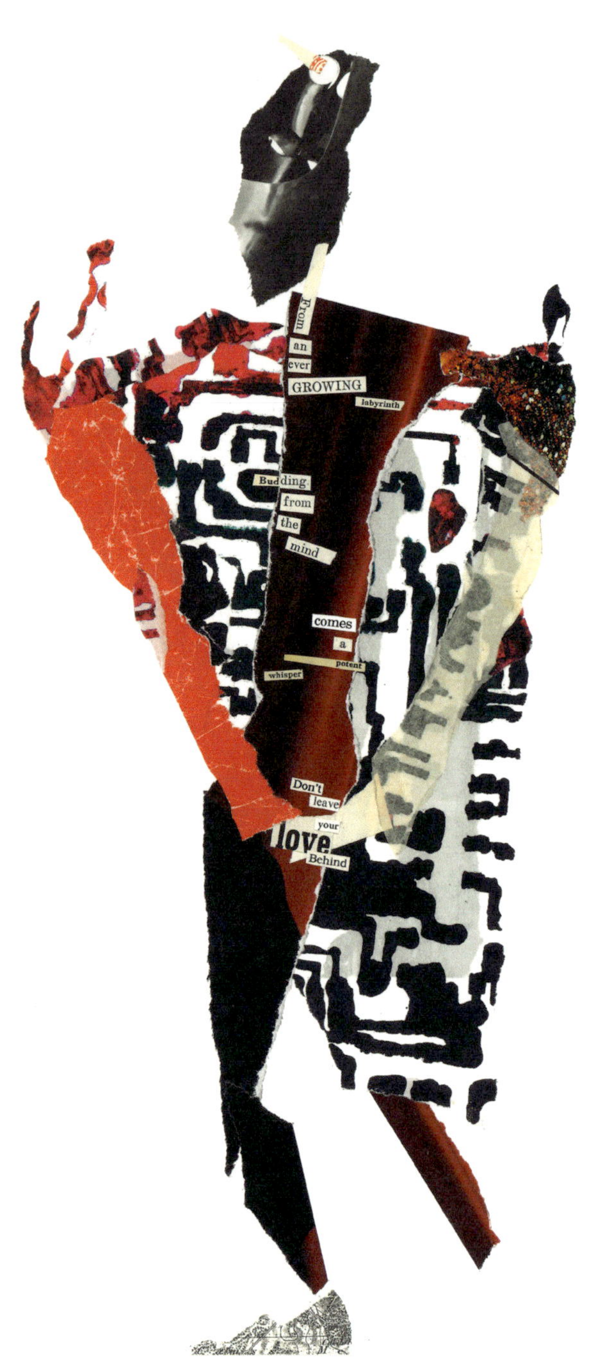
From
an
ever
GROWING
labyrinth
Budding
from
the
mind
comes
a
potent
whisper
Don't
leave
your
love
Behind

Table of Contents

Introduction

In July 2022, we joined a group of creatives at the artists' residency at Chateau d'Orquevaux, near Chaumont, France, meeting for the first time. One of us a poet, the other a collage maker. At first, it wasn't clear if common ground would emerge beyond the residency's unique experience. However, as the days progressed, we engaged in writing and collaging, discovering the freedom to explore alternative possibilities, envisioning new approaches, and pushing boundaries. This led us to explore the interactive potential of our respective mediums in the form of a collaboration.

At the Chateau, this evolved into an experiment in live action writing and collaging: the poet scribbled lines, tearing them from her notebook to create literary fragments alongside the collagist's pile of papers. The collagist improvised with these poetic gestures, crafting collages uniquely inspired by their interaction. Two pieces were created in this manner at the Chateau, marking the culmination of our collaboration there. However, thoughts about the potential for a longer-term creative connection began to surface, though the form it might take remained uncertain.

With a new-found desire to collaborate ignited, and the residency now a memory, the question arose: what next? During our time in France, amid the clutter of a collagist's studio, strange collage characters began to emerge in a tiny graphic journal made from paper scraps. Walling had glimpsed these creations, but it was only after independently writing a prescient short poem that began "In the labyrinth of wind…" that the idea of characters roaming within a labyrinth took shape. In response, Knights crafted the first character to enter this maze-like world, the 'Choreographer'. Over the past two years, Walling penned 51 poems while Knights fashioned 51 collage characters from his assortment of paper scraps. The creative flow worked in both directions, with some poems inspiring collages and vice versa. Additionally, there was a singular instance where they crossed disciplines: the poet created a collage titled Boatman in response to a poem by the collagist.

Continuing to connect and collaborate, we found joy in weaving our distinct artistic voices together. Through poems and collages, we discovered a harmonious dialogue where creativity flowed freely across disciplines. Our journey exemplifies the enduring power of collaboration, breathing life into new ideas and forging deeper connections through shared artistic exploration.

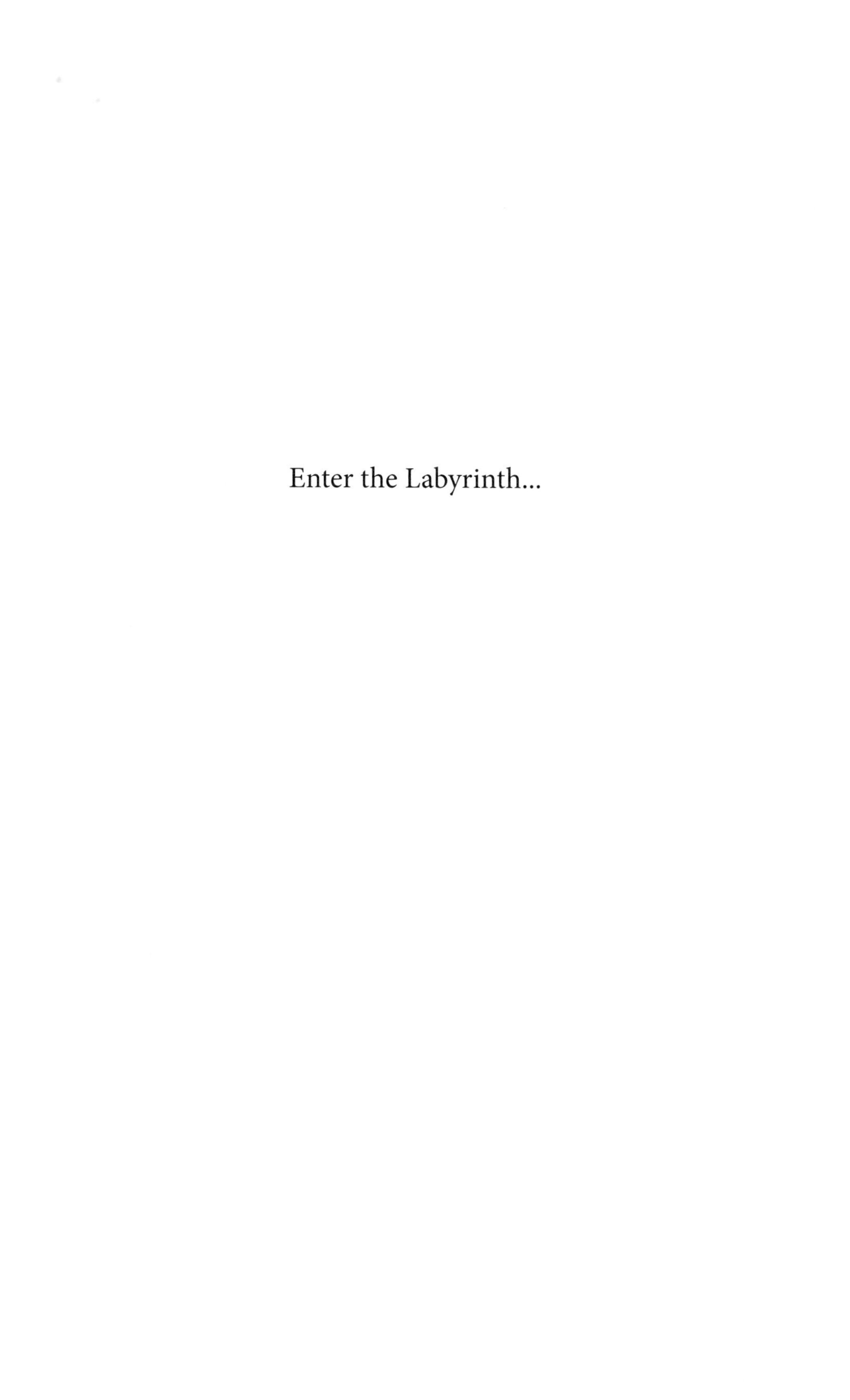

Enter the Labyrinth...

Choreographer

In the labyrinth of wind,
Walls extend to the clouds.
There is no way up,
There is no way down.

There are clues to survival,
Passed silently through the air.
Sent from other travellers,
Sent from here to there.

Messages come in scrambled,
Connecting builds the key.
Holding on to creation,
Is what will set one free.

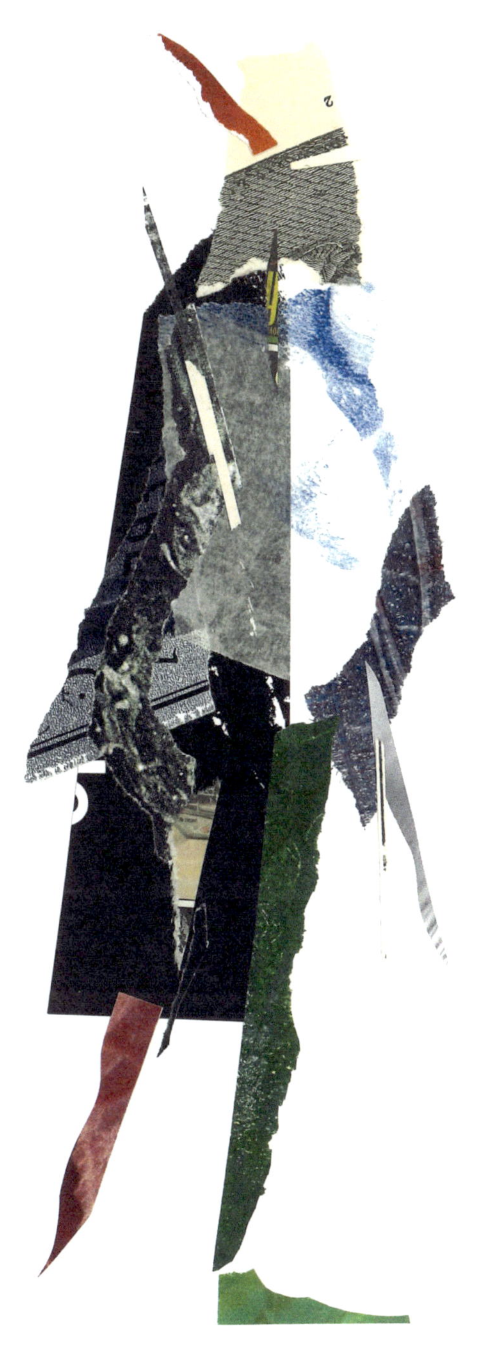

Fate Connector

Whatcha soul doin?
Floating around,
In its jellyfish state,
Bumpin into others
Connecting inside fate?

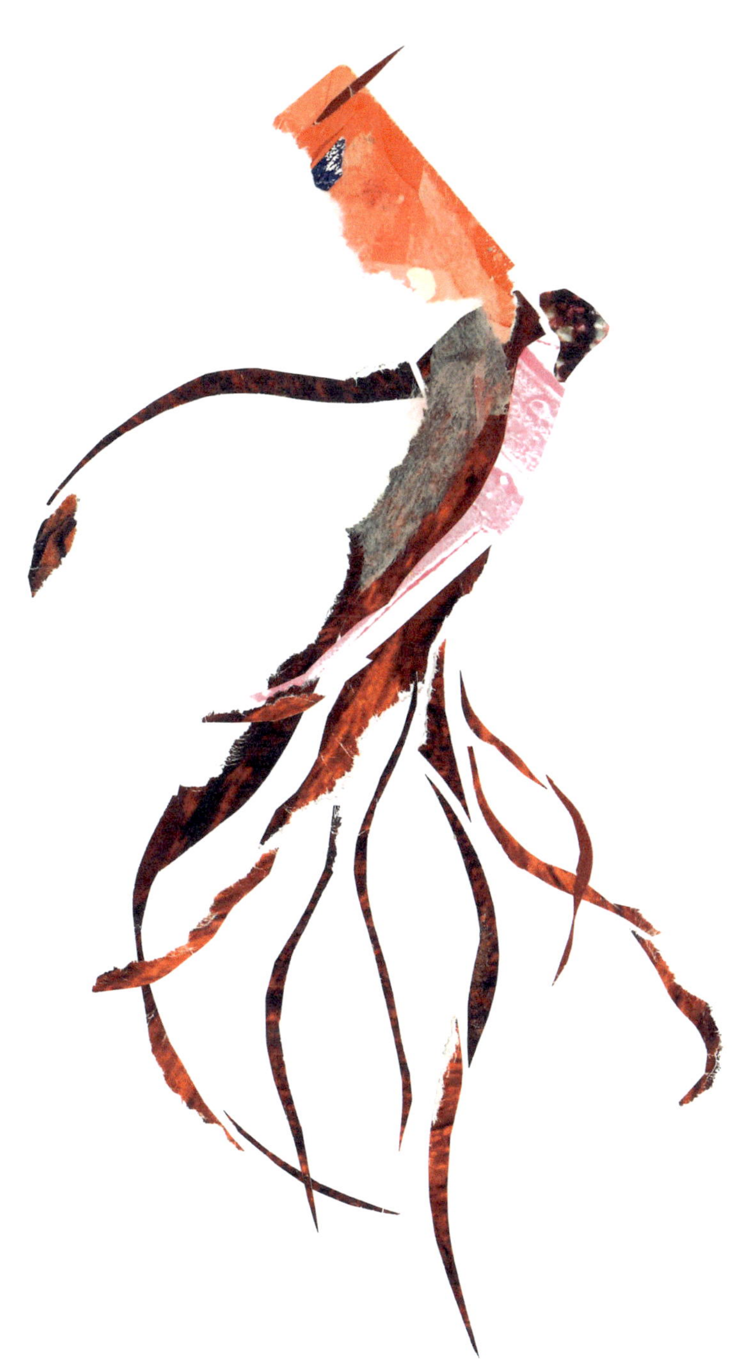

Immortal

I tried to become immortal,
In every way I could.
The validation killed me,
Never understood.

I wrote my soul in futile ground,
Just to watch it wash away.
Waiting for the tide to come,
In absolute dismay.

I have stood upon sacred land,
Feeling the air stand still.
Listening to medieval music,
Wondering of its will.

When I lay within a sun stream,
Surrounded by pure calm.
I recognize my place here,
Knowing it's but a song.

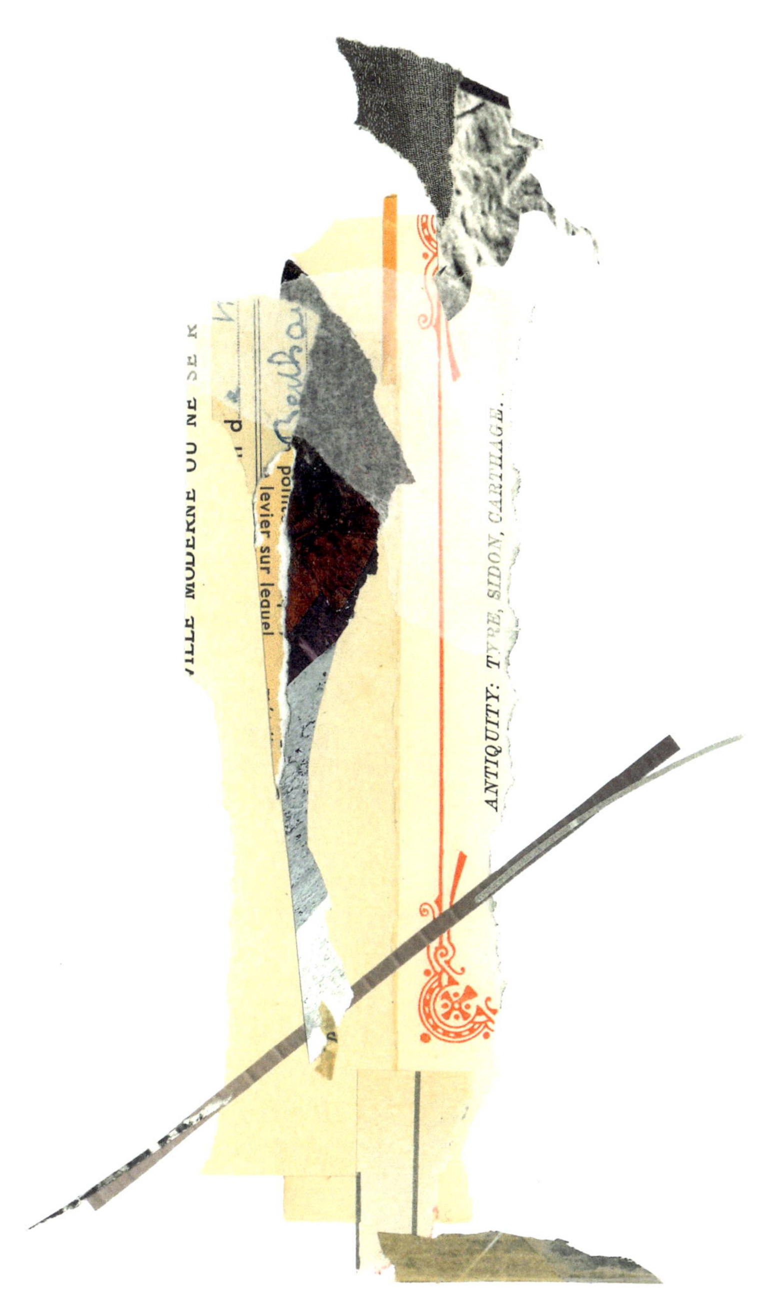
VILLE MODERNE OU NE SE
levier sur lequel
ANTIQUITY: TYRE, SIDON, CARTHAGE.

Beauty Blurrer

How does one capture beauty,
And hold it in a vase,
Bottling up each rose petal,
In solitary grace?

How does one capture beauty,
The shimmer on the sea,
Freezing up each flicker,
Dismissing its calm plea?

I've tried to capture beauty,
Hold it in my words,
Confine it on my paper,
The meaning became blurred.

One can not capture beauty,
It will cease to exist,
When trapped in mundaneness,
Its essence can't persist.

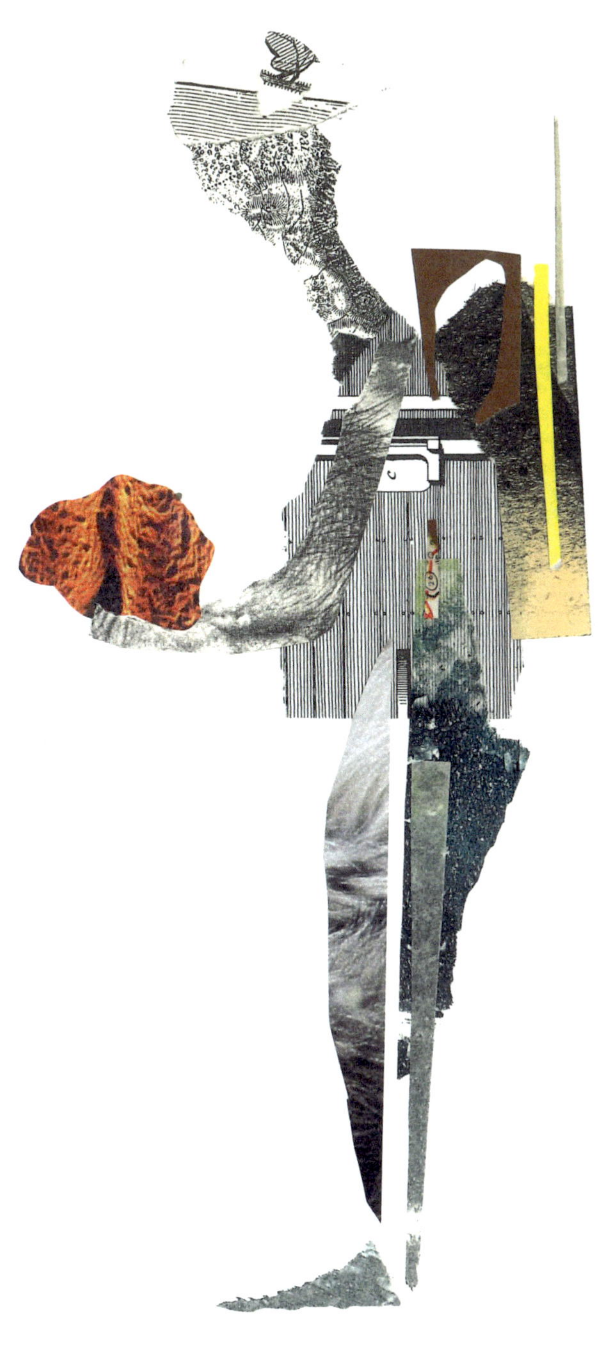

Lawnkeeper

A thousand words,
Sit on a blade of grass.
Hovering forward,
Pushing back.

Capturing songs,
That float through the wind.
Soaking up stardust,
Breathing it in.

Searching for chaos,
A return to the source.
Opening portals,
To forests lost.

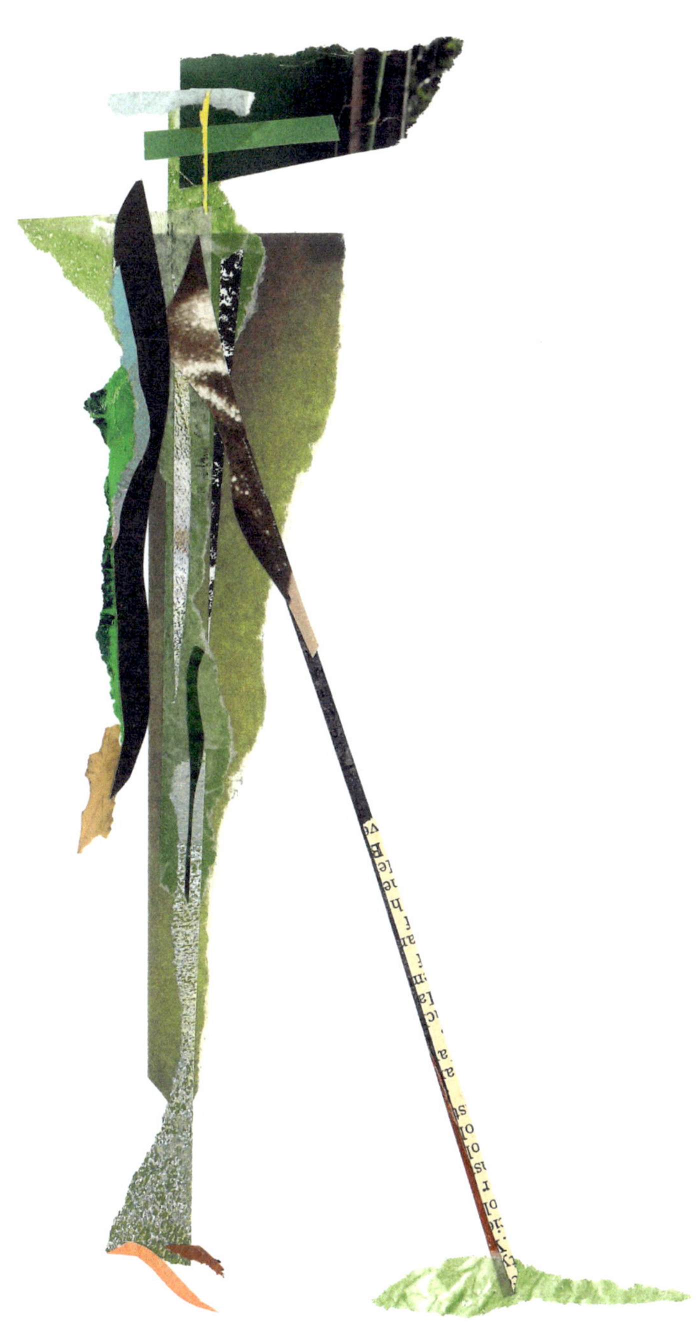

Time Holder

A traveller bent on

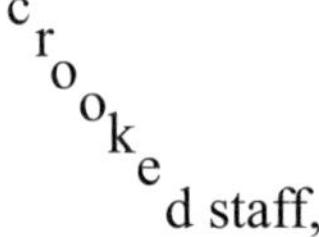

Weaved along a jilted path.
He stood a moment like

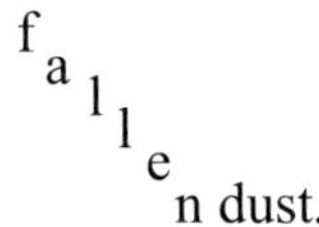

Shaken from the essence of trees.

A lady sat upon that path,
And spotted the

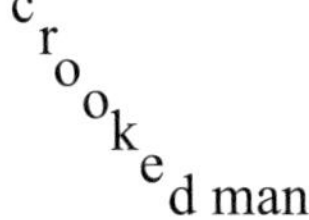

She said "dear sir? What
is that
you carry in your
hand?"

"I have time in my hand,
dear woman"
And if you remember
well
I was your greatest
lover
Into a pit I

f
e
l
l

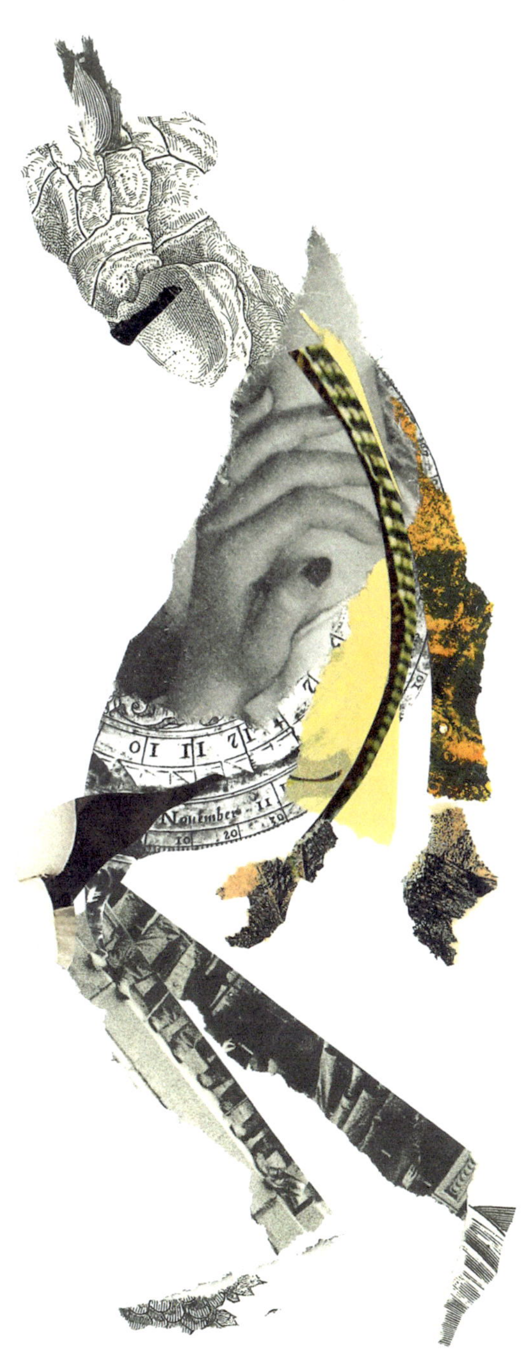
Nouember

Blip Dripper

Eyes turned toward
The heavens.

Wings stretching for
Temples overgrown.

- there are momentary blips -

Eyes drip stars
That fall like wishes
Landing on the lips
Of a lover.

- flickering heaven across
        every inch of their body -

There is danger
in the sky.

The sun caresses wax wings
With the reminder of their futility
Sending them crashing to earth.

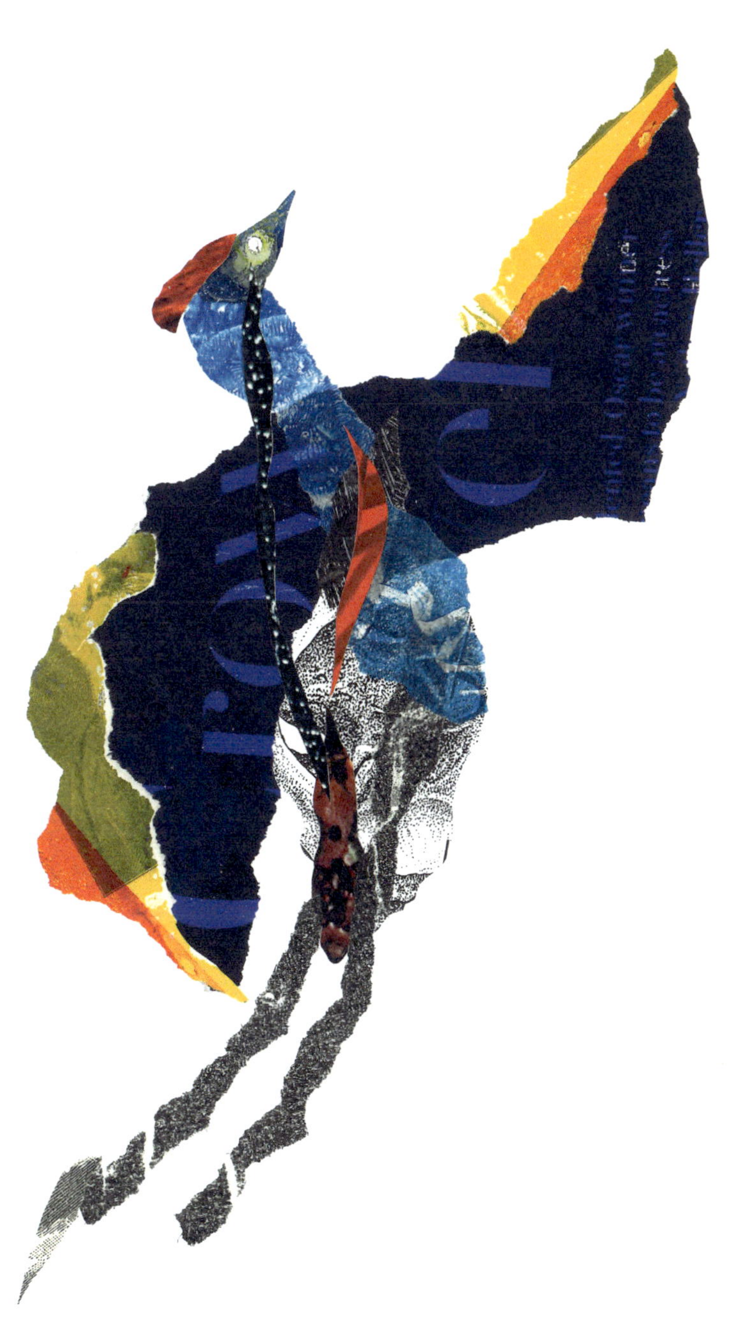

Zorlama

I lost my mind on the 21
{The devil came and snatched it}
Fed it to the nearest car
Laughing at the rhetoric.

Is there time to grab a snack,
On my way down south?
Absolutely, my dear!
But that requires a mouth.

One that you no longer have
{Because of the said snatching}
So close your eyes and buckle in
For this moment is really happening.

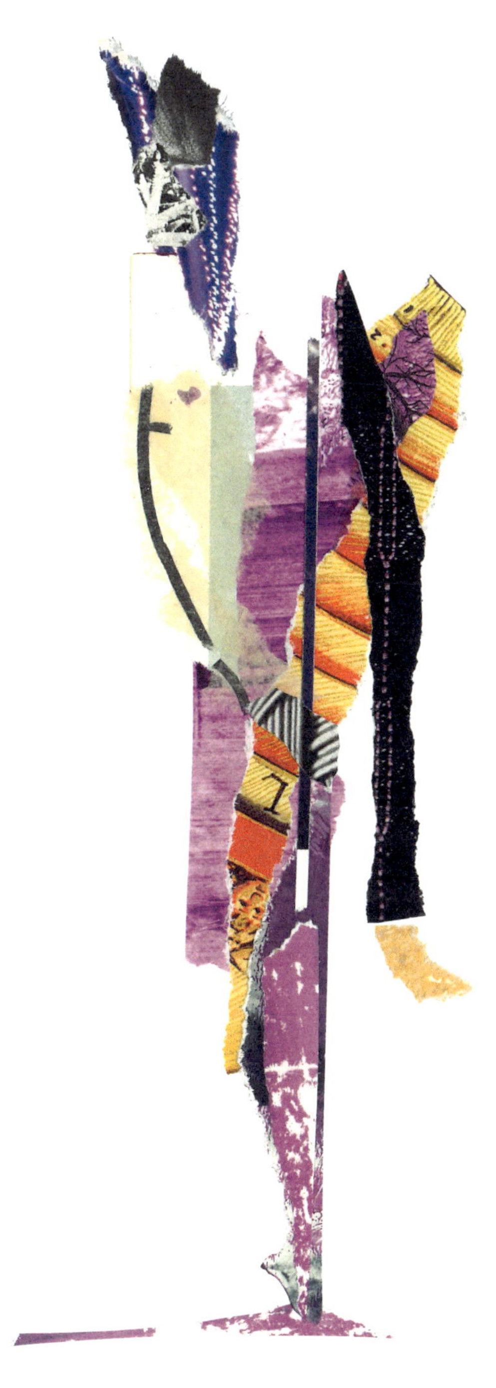

Lost Self

In the balloon room
- we sat -
Smacking balloons
- fragments through gaps -

“I write around the edges of the paper”

If you’re not organizing chaos, what are you doing really?

From the time before,
There was speculation
- floating through the silence
                    a calling
                      one may say -
A sense that magic existed
And that music cured all.

When the flatness came
It settled hard
In cracks of the old building
Crumbling the last piece that stood.

An outline still exists
Ready to be restored
To the splendour
Of what it was always intended to be.

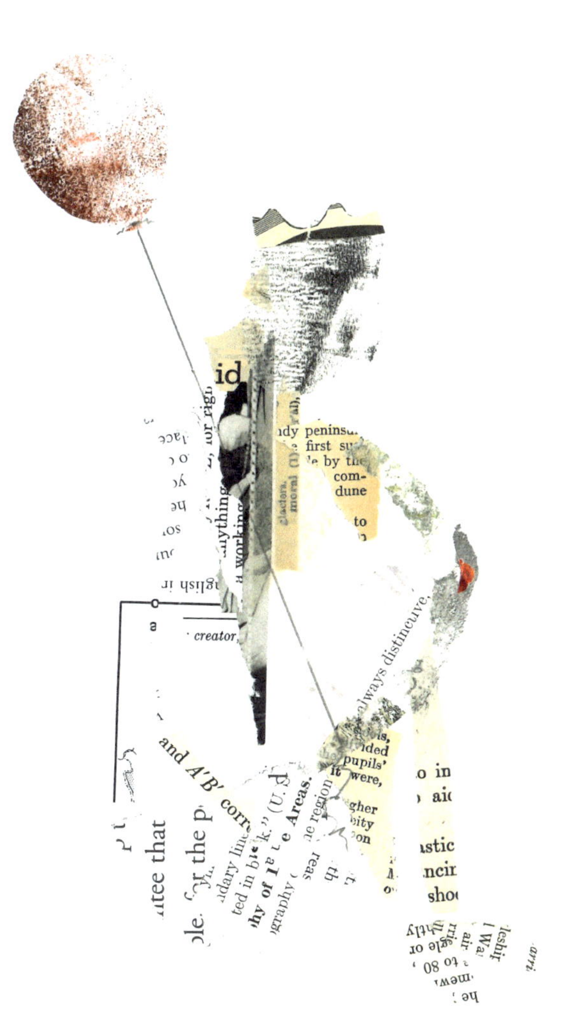

Pink Punk

There's a dance and a flow
An I don't know
As she shouts
Yet, is not heard.

Higher she goes
Onto tippy toes
To rise above the crowd.

A bellowing scream
Enhances the dream
She is the essence of a swirl.

Standing tall
No cares at all
With movement like the wind.

Gagged no more
Never again to crawl
A fierce, compiled queen.

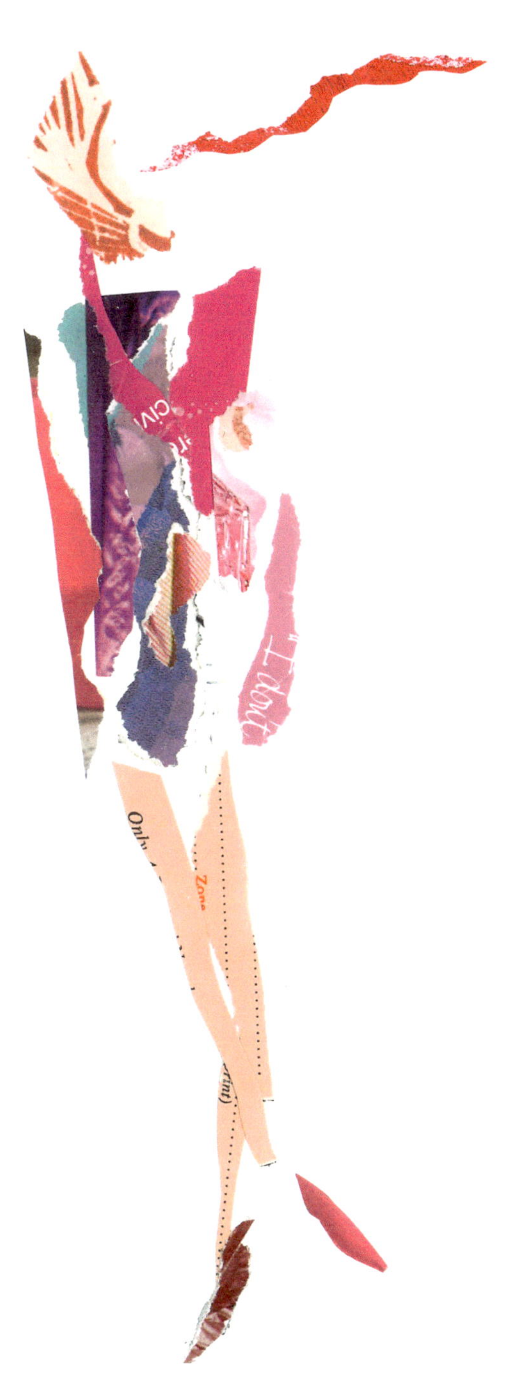

I don't
Only

Board Jumper

I beckon you to know yourself,
Capture stardust for your own.
Plot until you follow through,
A memorable mixture of what is true.
Wear your heart upon your head,
Create a world made for you.
Fill it with deep desires,
Feel the rush through and through.
In a world of subjective rules,
Challenge those who made the game.
For it was never made for you,
It was meant for the mundane.
Escape the board of numbed design,
And jump into the infinite blue.

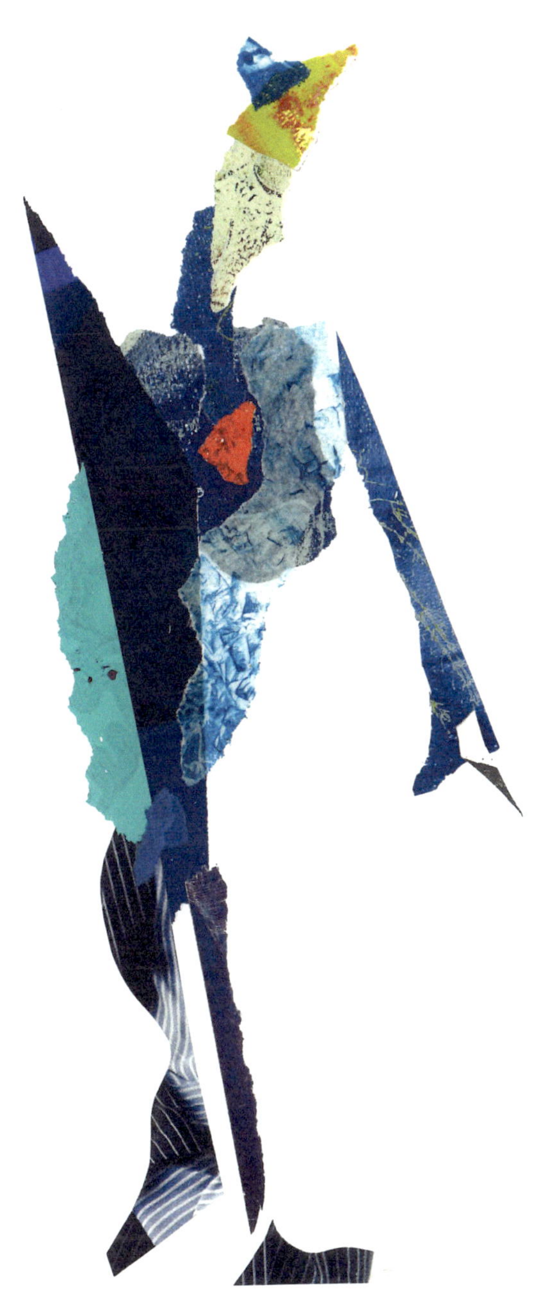

Gemini

A wistful wanderer,
Searches the sky -
Through the frenzy,
Sits Gemini -

The air is thick,
The blanket black -
Light shines in,
Through a tiny crack.

Eyes with a numb culpability -
Recognizes a concussed,
Noble vulnerability.

Imprinted soul to fight the dark,
Inside the choice to disembark.

A clever and clear choice appears
To open the eyes
And clear the ears.
To hold on wistfully in the night
To search the sky
For transcendent light.

What is now - will always be
For the cloth came from eternity

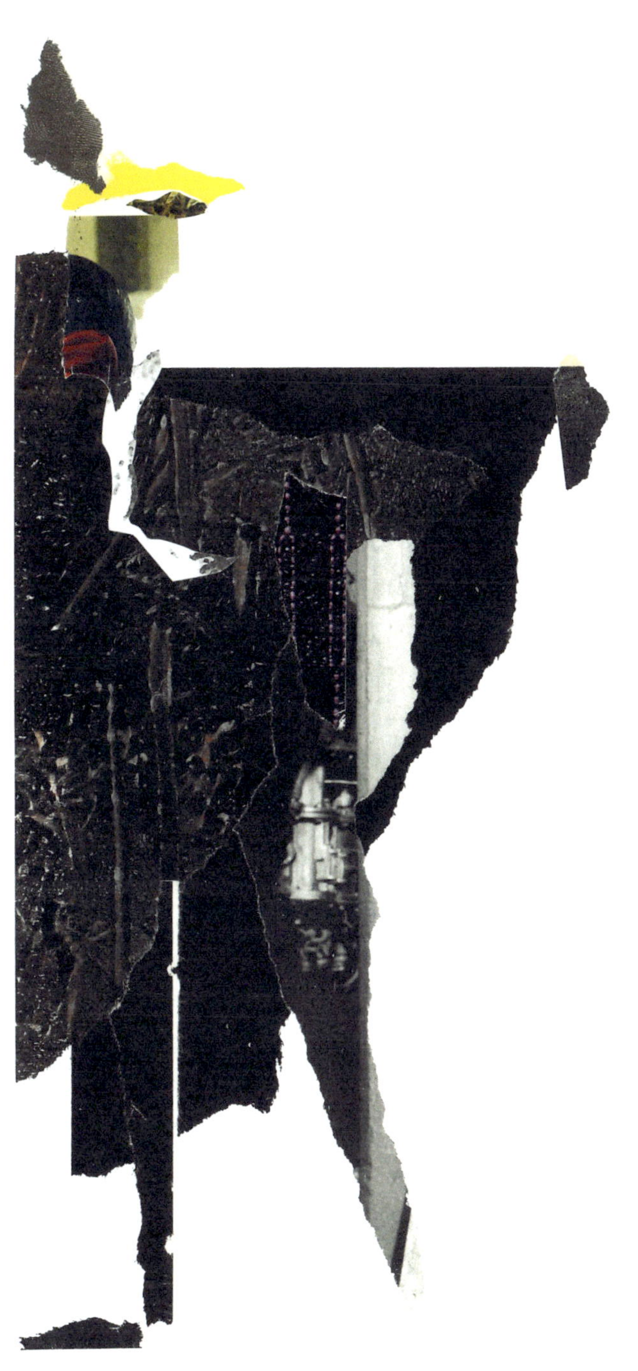

Executioner

Take me all and look for more,
Rotted now to rooted core.
Your poison long spread into me,
All to try and help you breathe.

All is none for one is you,
Long you've waited for me to rue.
The day has come and you smile bright,
I almost forgot that deadly bite.

Altered and evaded well,
The blame is mine, you can "tell".
Not your fault and whatever else,
You tell yourself so no pain is felt.

A master you are,
At this dark art.
My soul is slain,
It's broke apart.

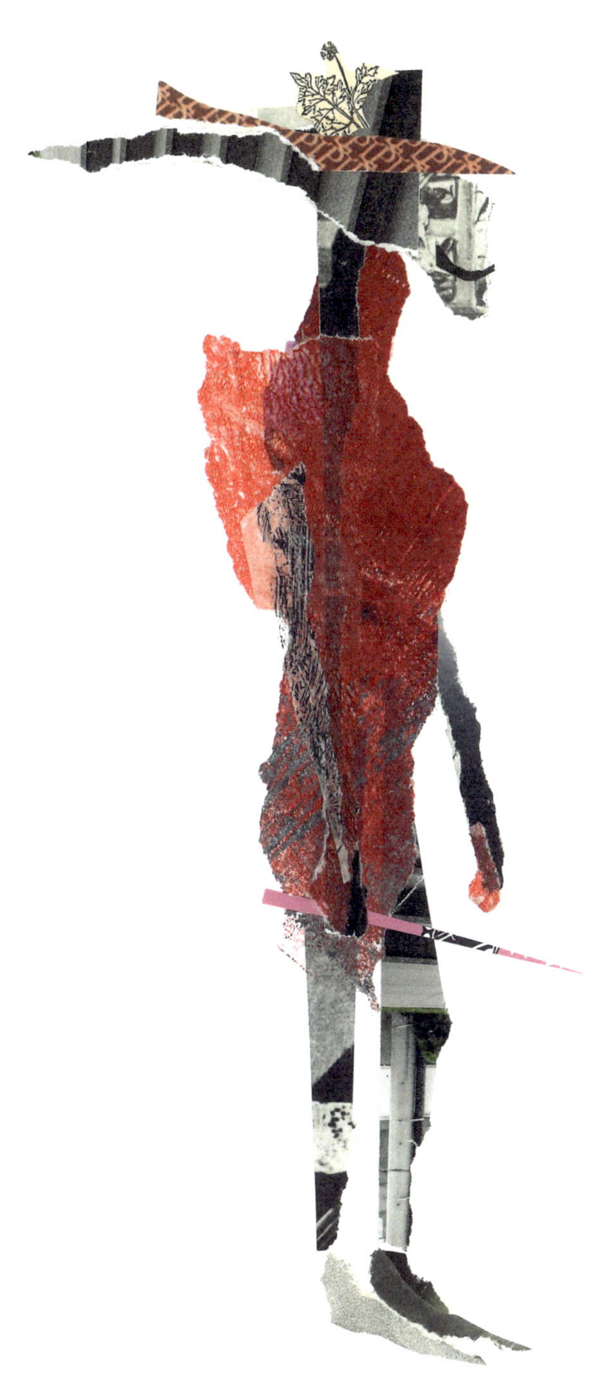

Boatman

Where does my consciousness go when I die?
The same place my heaviness goes when I fly?

Does it lodge in the gap between upside and down,
or wait at the spot where the unicorn's found?

Is it there in the substance rejected by clouds,
or in lines left mysteriously on burial shrouds?

Does it hang above newborns in hopes of rebirth,
or ooze from the backsides of worms in the earth?

Will my consciousness linger in cremation ash
or inhabit the void after thunder has flashed?

Can it make itself known even though I'm not there,
issue in silence from a daydreamers' stare?

Or offer inflection to the sound of a sigh
when perplexed by perennial questions of why?

Can my consciousness be without body and breath?
Does it ever survive the finality of death?

It can't just evaporate, surely that's wrong,
be there for a lifetime then suddenly… gone?

What of the memories, the suffering, the love,
devotion to causes and powers from above?

Is all this just grist for a mechanized mill
grinding up matter into meaningless swill?

Or should I be hopeful for something in store
where consciousness changes to something much more?

Becoming a star in the night sky perhaps,
and shining its light until time has elapsed?

Is that such an immodest hope for my soul,
to have unending luminescence as a goal?

Forgive me if I'm not impressed with the state
of philosophers' reflections on our ending date

Response to my question is jaded at best,
and met with disinterest or clichés when pressed.

So, once more, where does my consciousness go
when my last expiration ceases to flow?

Now answer the question you dithering fuck,
yes you, dear reader, don't just pass the buck!

If you cannot figure it nobody can
'cos your gonna die like the rest of the clan,

be entropic blobs of organic matter,
devoid of identity, ego and chatter.

Where does your consciousness go when you die,
when you sing out that final whimpering cry?

Take it from me it's a humbling question
so, at this point I'm welcoming any suggestion.

Just don’t give me nonsense of heaven or grace,
or materialist notions of leaving no trace

Now you can see me, then, now you do not,
is that all there is to completing our lot?

I’m perplexed and astounded at how much we know,
yet have no fucking clue where consciousness goes.

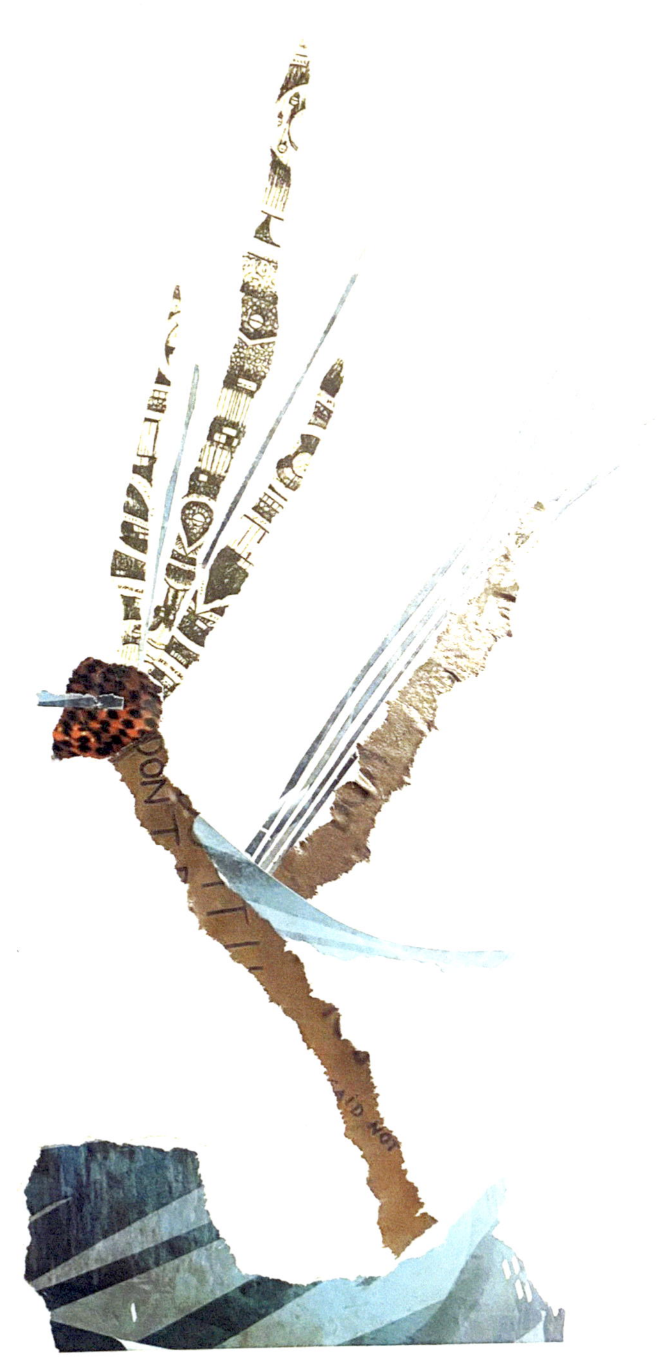

Seraphina

I don’t want to die,
I just want to feel,
Just want to feel,
Want to feel,
To feel,
Feel.

I don’t want to die,
I just want to heal,
Just want to heal,
Want to heal,
To heal,
Heal.

I don’t want to die.

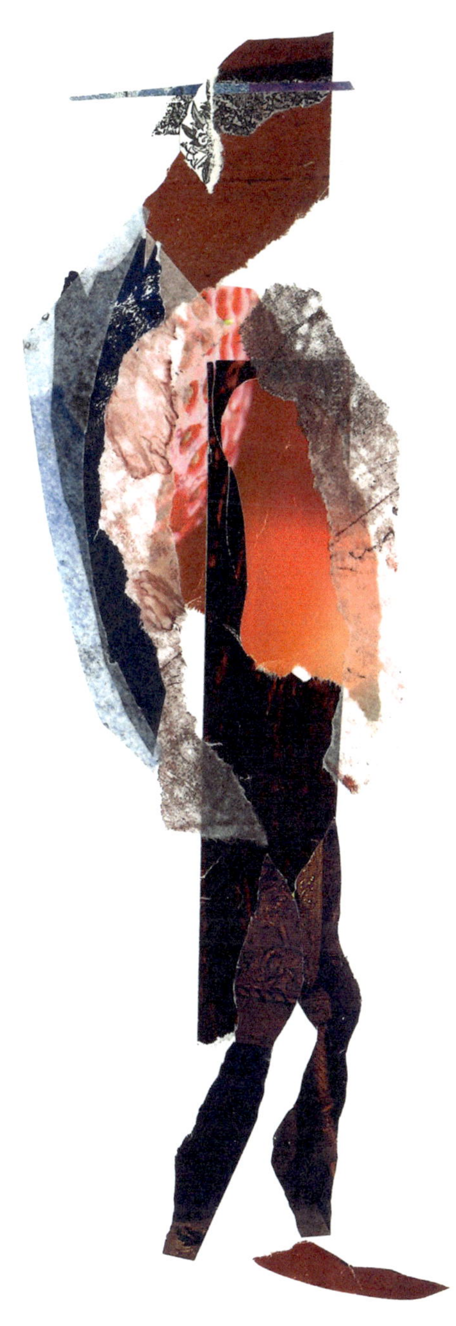

Dainty Foot

In the outer box
There stems a clatter.
A clickity clack
Of baser matter.
Tiny hoof feet
Against plaster
Dancing into the ever after.

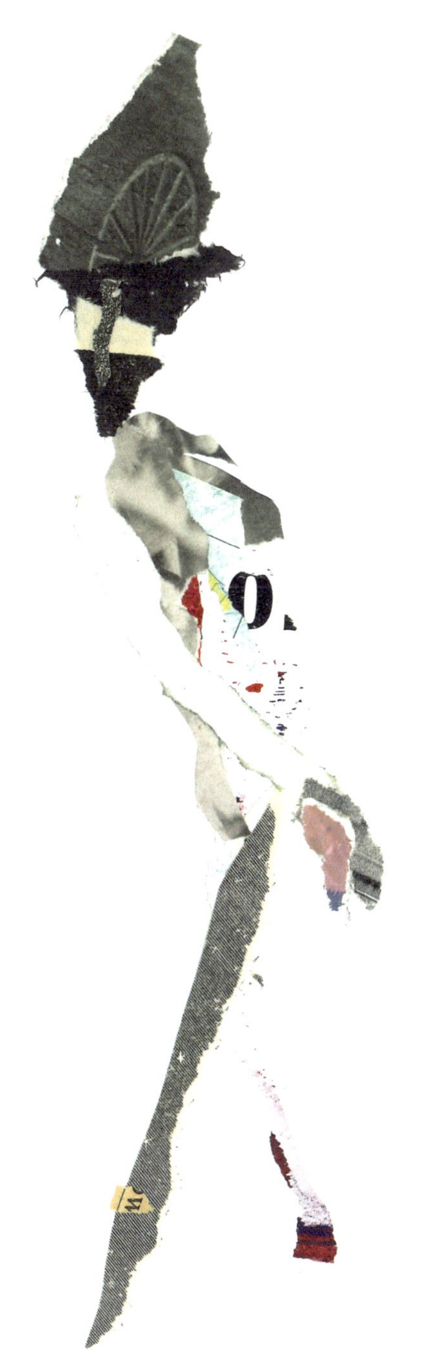

the outer bo

Soldier

In the clouds,
And through the air,
Shadows captured everywhere.
Holding tight,
To the closest breeze,
Pulling false memories,
From the trees.

- a whisper -

Sent from here to there,
Dangling in his forward stare.
Firm brow straight,
Head held high.
Marching along the longest sigh.

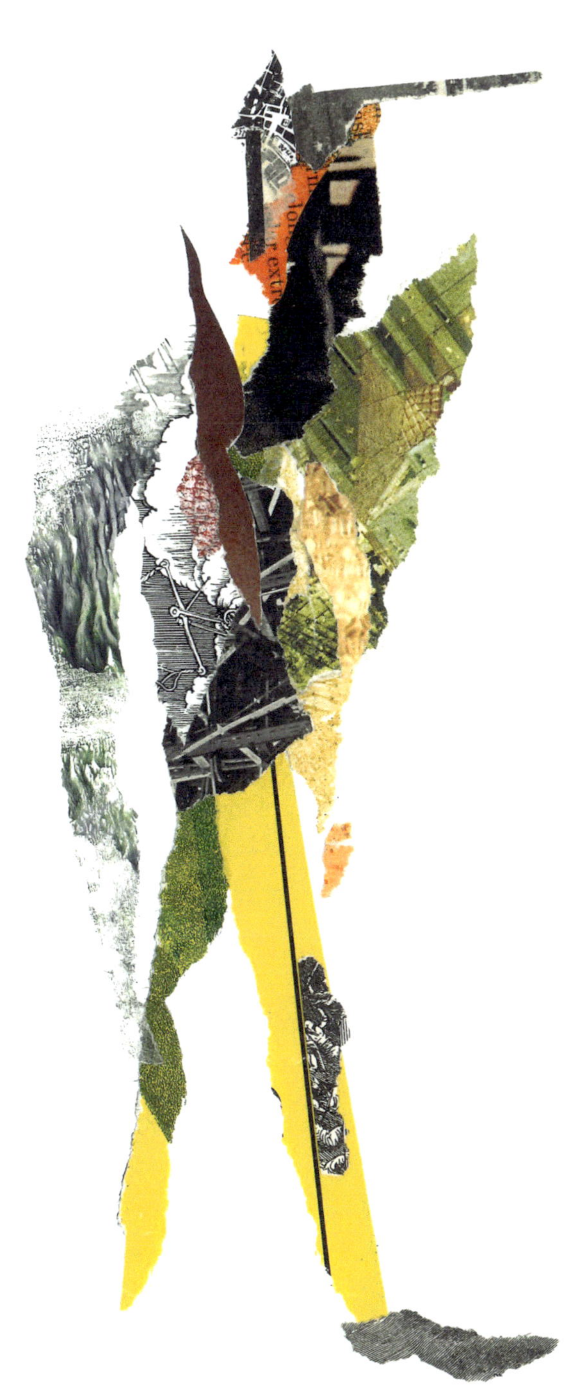

Beekeeper

There's a longevity to nectar,
Though it nests in borrowed time.
A surge through commonality,
Searching for moonshine.

Trembling in his being,
With a forward facing stare.
Reaching for the others,
While living in nowhere.

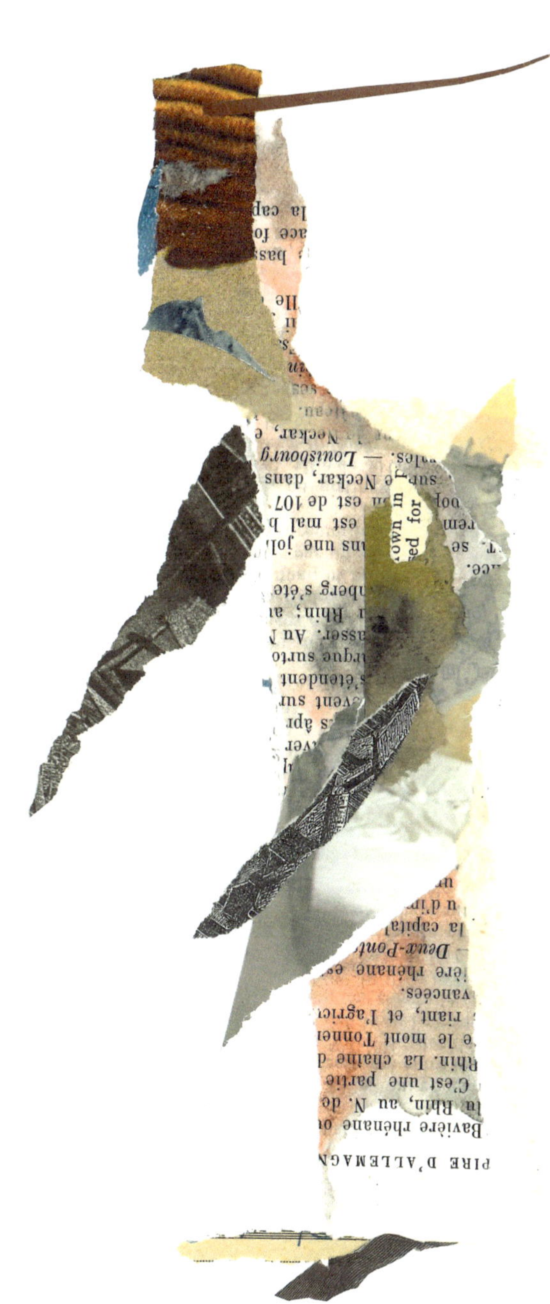

Cin

An artifice of pure gold,
Was caste within a diamond mould,
And placed up high upon its place,
Where glory shone on its shiny face.
All that saw it praised its sight,
They stared up high at its glorious light.

When one day something twisted yearned,
Building within that golden urn.
It festered and grew from inside the glory,
And forged its own darker story.
Although the outside shone with splendour,
Deeper lurked a dark attender.

With pressure building up so strong,
The worshippers heard not the dark song.
Which leaked and played its whispering tune,
Then stood up tall howling at the moon.
And crept out fully from that crack,
Attaching itself to an unsuspecting back.

Which writhed in pain and absorbed the dark,
A new adventure on which to embark.
Happy for a mobile host,
It corrupted no more that golden ghost.

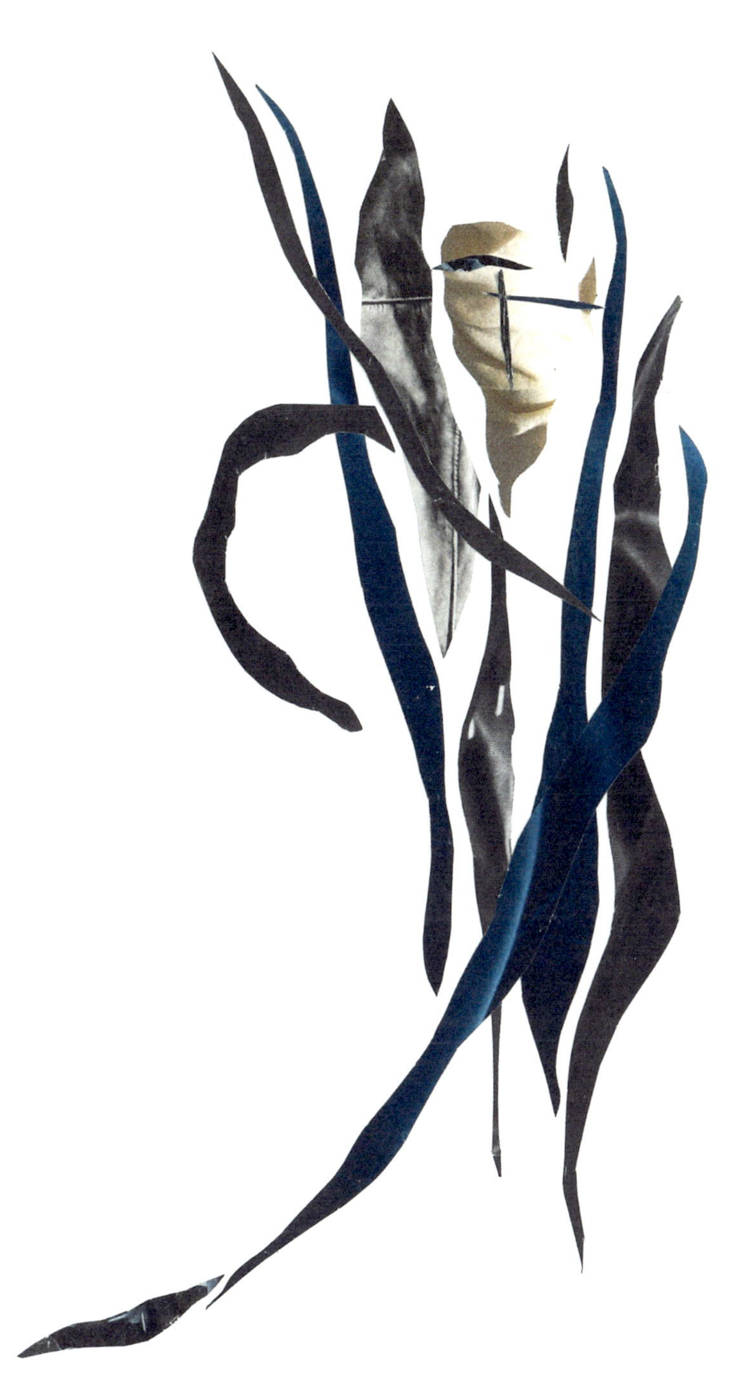

Collector

There he stands
Behind the trees
Judging you
        And judging me
Waiting for his "authentic"
Moment of attack.

He senses a vibration in the air -
        To be fair
                The care was taken -
He has no concern
For those living in the light.

Hiding amongst the shadows -
With his bag full of souls,
Orchestrating a hold.
Knowing that the sun can bring
On worlds,
As they hold the essence of humanity.

One without judgement
Of misfits and moments

"I can not let that be"
Thinks he.

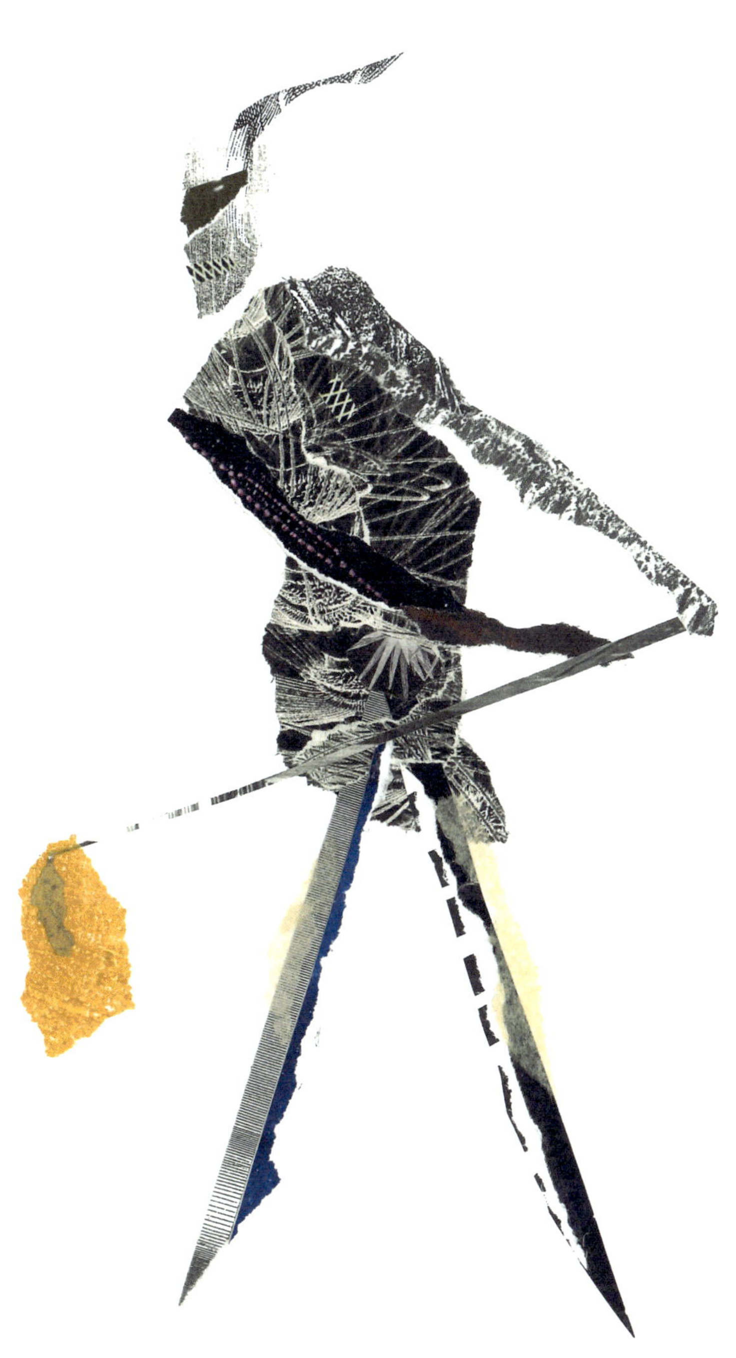

Arachne

Word spinner,
Word weaver,
Arachne caught in a cage.

Devious to the core,
Came about it naturally,
Always having to explain.

Open the cage,
Unleash Pandora's box,
Purple world of pleasure,
Never understanding forever.

Glimpse into the unknown,
Tell me what is home.

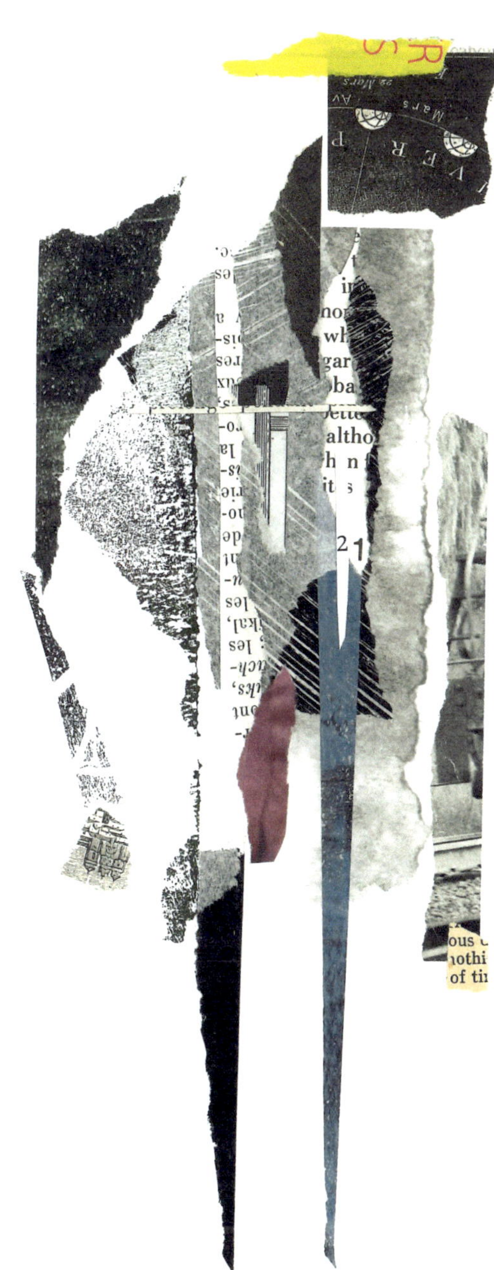

Archer

He shot an arrow into a tree
And what he did devise
Was that motion must not exist
And thus it was comprised
Of moments suspended
Loosely hanging there in space
And that humans are but fragments
Of some nonexistent place.

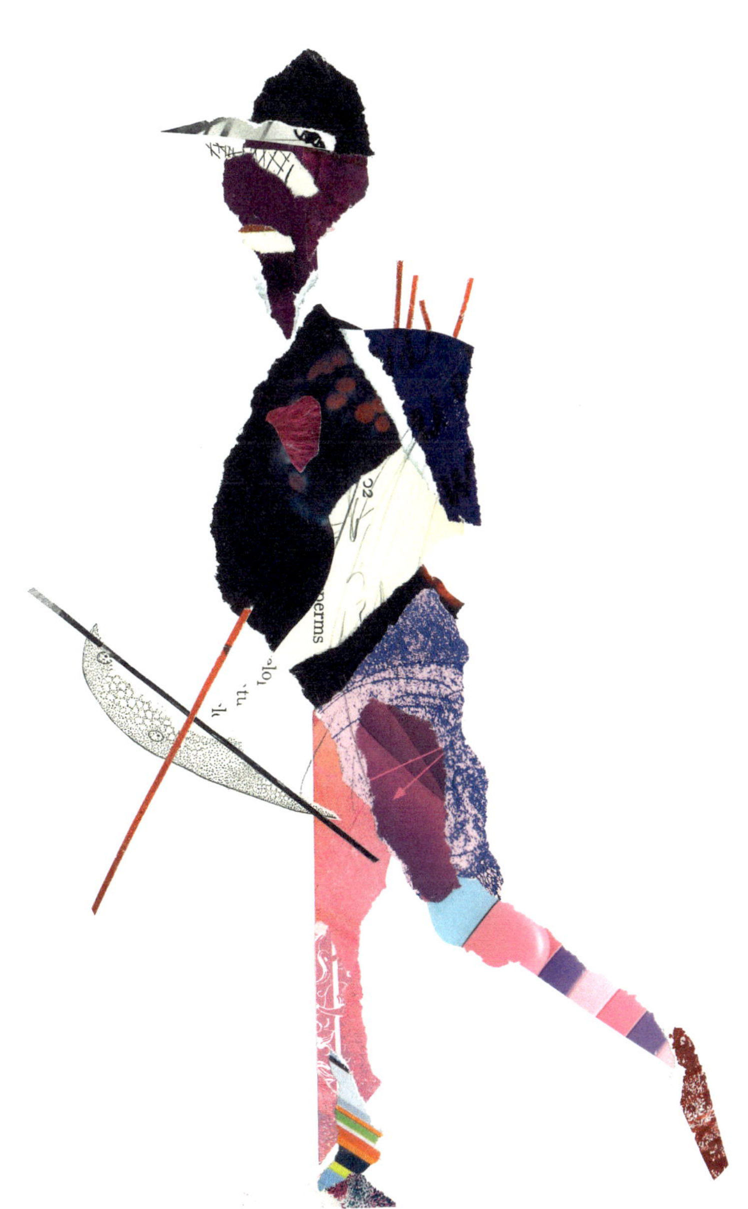

Sprite

To the world that doesn't hear me,
From echoes of the heart.
From deep within the forest,
Addressing what's been chopped apart.

The monsters in the forest,
(The ones you know exist)
Wrap around the senses,
They slide inside and twist.

As I am from the forest folk,
I hold a bit of wild.
It's my nature to defy order,
Chaos does not favour the mild.

I'm here to share a vision,
Transport you to the spot.
The roots that I am standing on,
Is the scene of a battle, just fought.

A monster has been slaughtered,
(The one that tore you apart)
With a shard of blue plucked from the sky,
Shattering its heart.

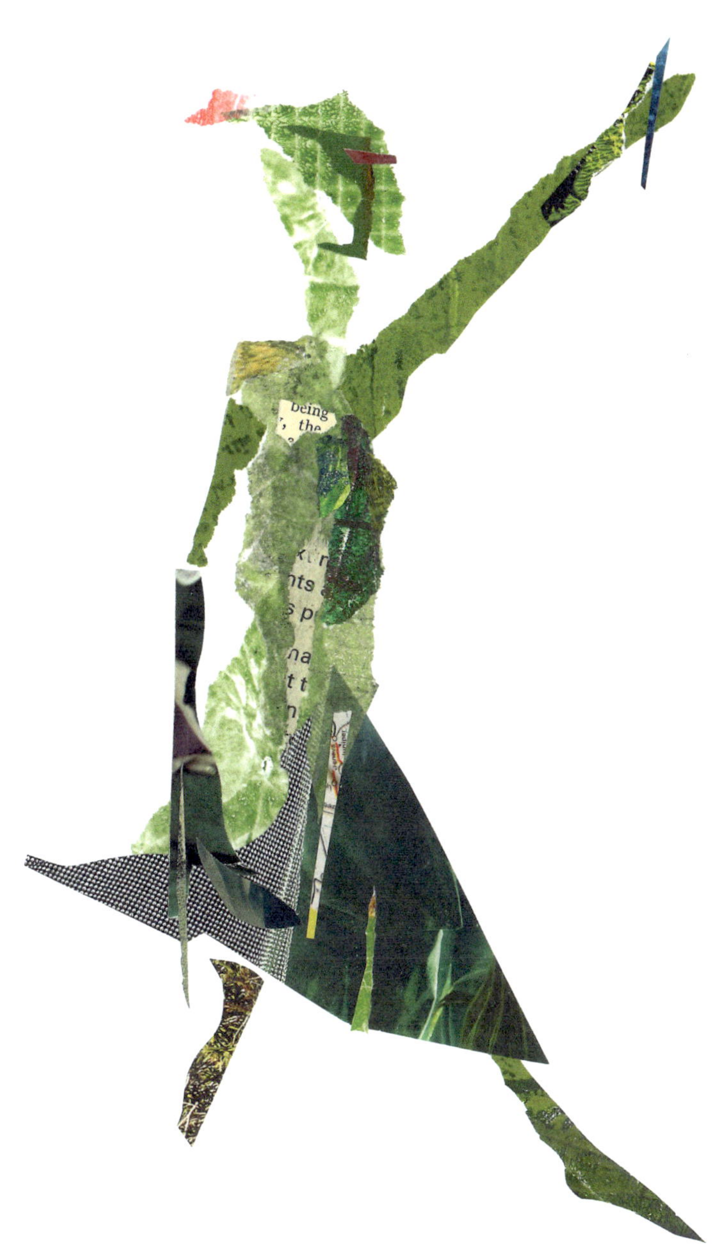
being
, the

Almost Naked

I am not who I used to be,
Yet I always am -
Skating along reality's line,
Elvish in my being.
I walk head high,
With mask down low,
Consumed memories only I see.
Crowded,
Tangled,
Wet,
Messes,
Of what I feel is free.
A question of conscience comes,
Flitting in and out.
I loudly whisper into the maze,
As I silently shout.
I am not who I used to be,
Yet I always am -

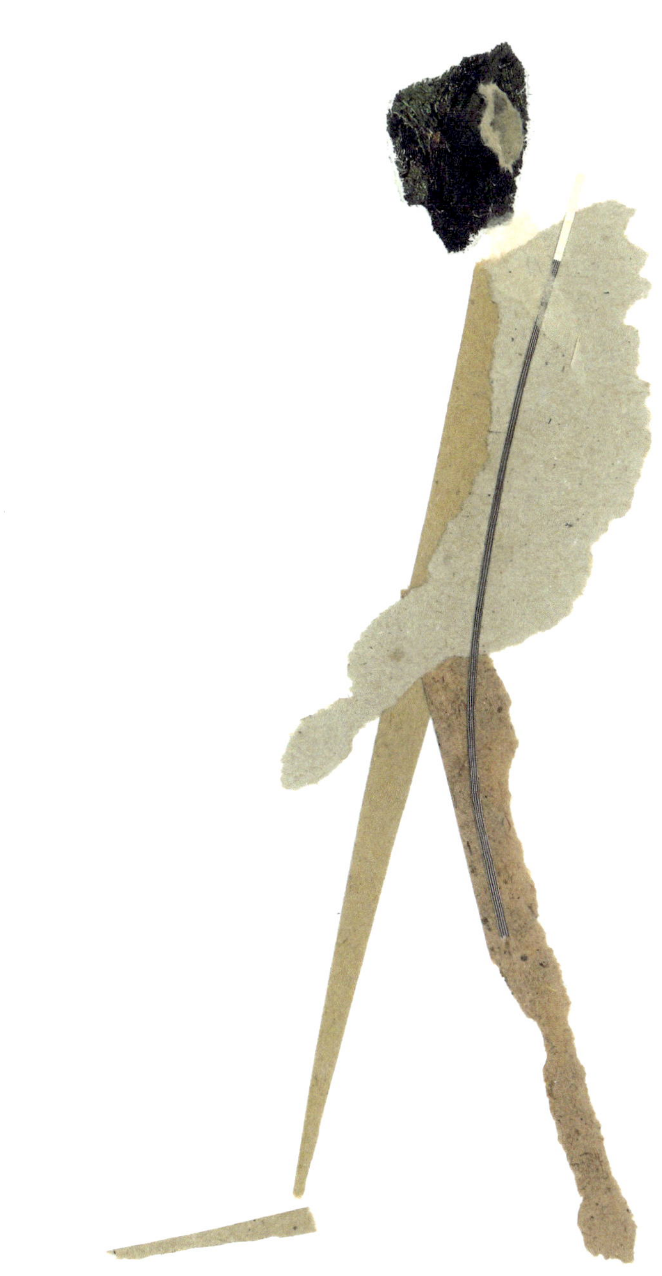

Inquisitor

Truth seeking (full truth) is an active and confusing challenge
Where one has to (belonging openly) engage
With constant (stretch of the mind) streams of input.

Yet (unfathomed) the order is irrelevant
The human (the human) is full and whole
When the mind becomes the catalyst (yearns to be full).

So (with) unleashed (dark desires) are lines of inquiry
And in those (unleashed) queries, seeds begin to worm
The roots (become alive) emerging from the shell.

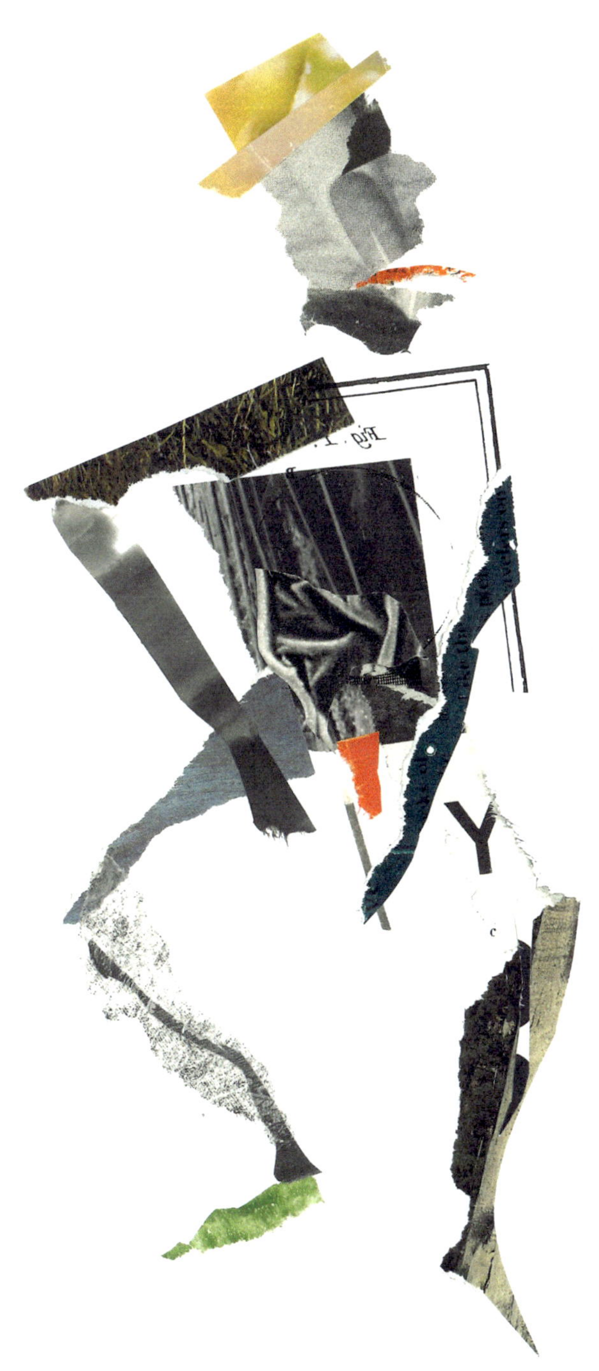

Silent Screamer

From thousands of nameless ancestors,
I hear the whisperous screams.
As the weight of being,
- no word -
Pushes me to my knees.
To say the name is to conspire,
While others speak in vain.
Complain and hear the roars,
Of those who hold the reins.

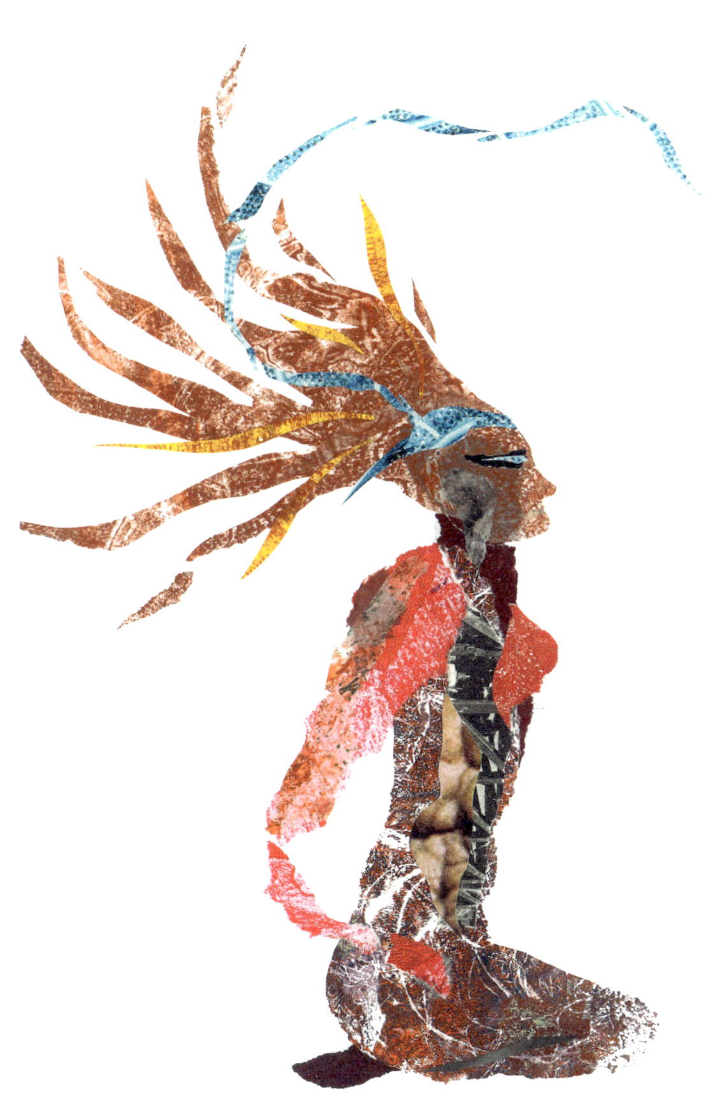

Ghost Leaf

I ache and I fold,
In leaves coloured gold,
Which reminds me of only you.

The house is still there,
It's empty and bare,
Everything smells untrue.

In one of the rooms,
Shakes the essence of you,
Vibrating in the air.

I gulp in lost sighs,
Closing my eyes,
A ghost of who I knew.

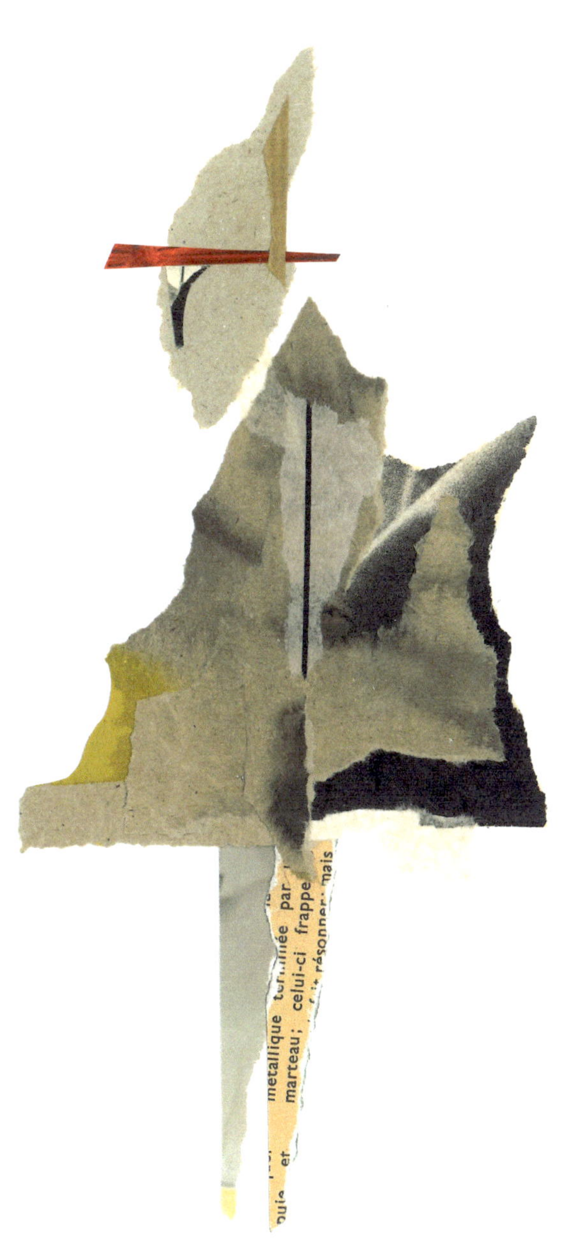
metallique par
et marteau; celui-ci frappe
résonner; mais

Possessed

Inconspicuous in the darkness of earth,
An ancient sacred one stirs.
Yielding a harvest in secret ministry,
As the quiet moonlight purrs.

Slumping to the surface,
A plane of reality concurrent to now.
Touching earth to cosmic mysticism,
The harvest shall have its plough.

Human bodies are temporary abodes,
In non-discriminatory overlap.
Directional forces take on the flow of life,
Clouds bellow loudly in an echoing clap.

The fallen man is now contaminated,
Intangible and tangible unite.
Cyclical directional forces,
Never having a chance to fight.

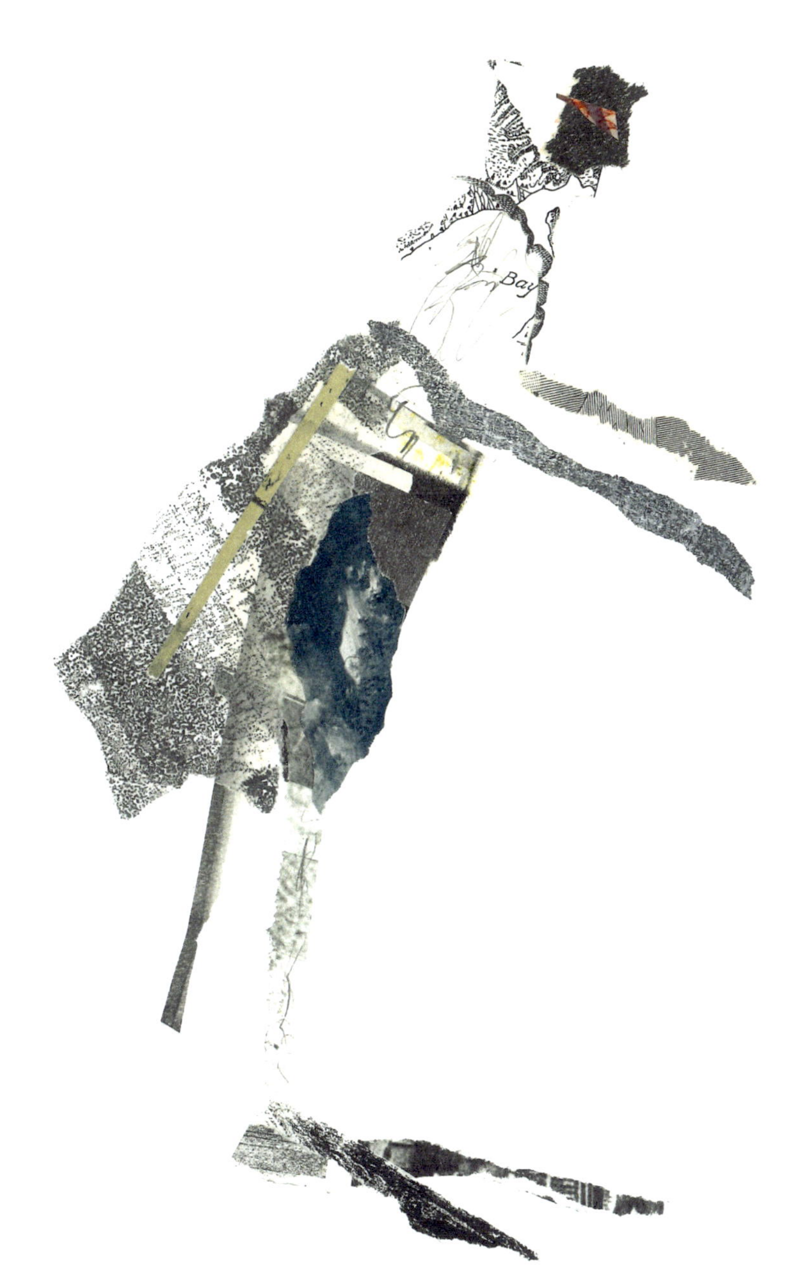
Bay

Windborne

I seek refuge from this matrix,
The one that is my mind.
Take me to the nether-land,
Show me where to hide.

Bring me to a meadow,
Swaddled in sun stream serene.
Lay me on a pastoral field,
Where only sparkle light is seen.

Surround me in the smell of love,
In all its many forms.
Whisper words of poetry,
Uncloud me from this storm.

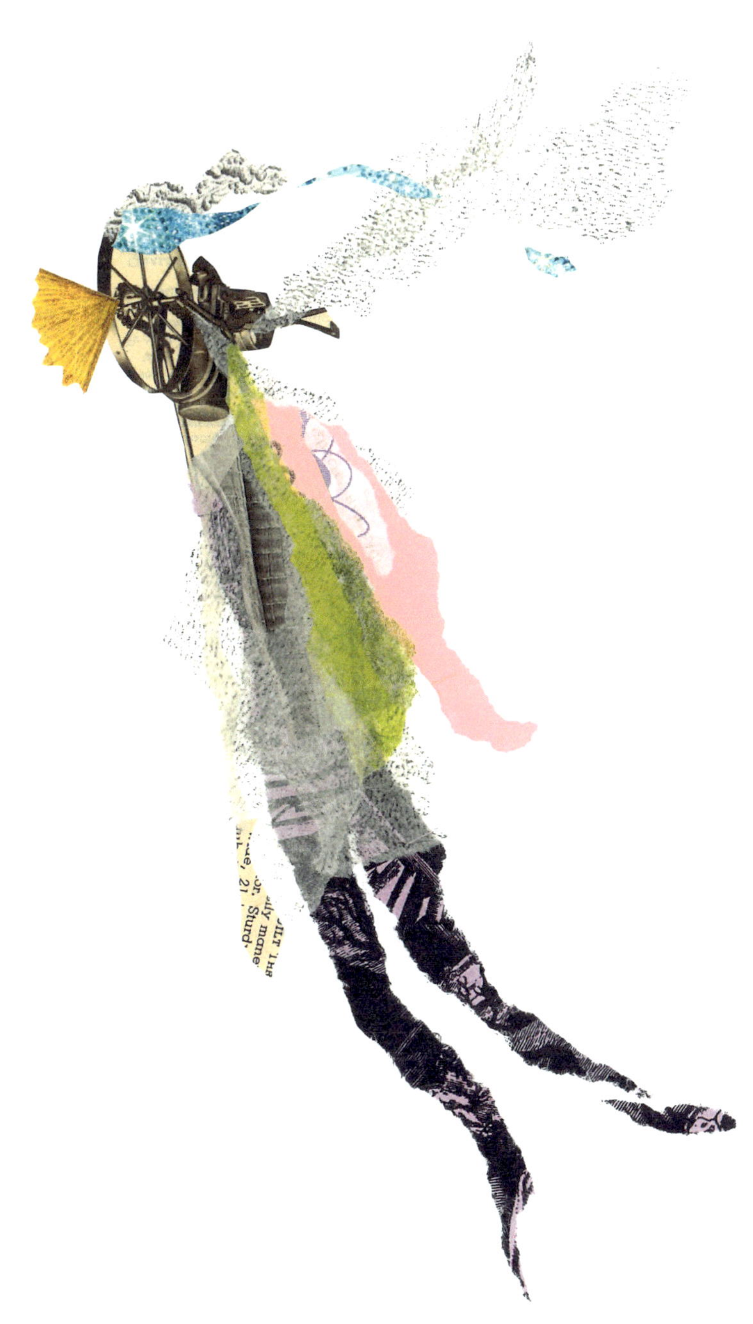

Mythologist

There's a tale to be told,
In the gaps and the folds,
Of whimsy and lovely lore.

Magic and air,
Just hanging there,
Placed in the evermore.

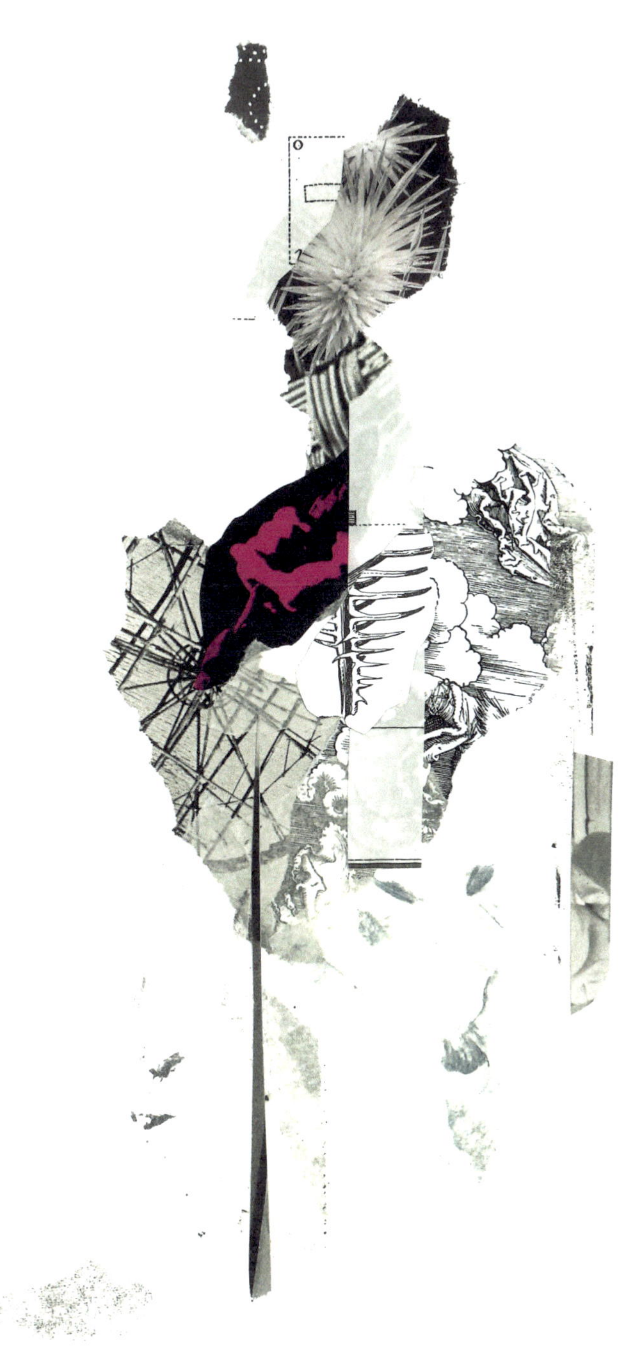

Fecit

Welcome to the inner workings
Of the swirly world!
Cut your way through,
It's a love rendezvous.
Here's a formal welcome,
Come in! Come in!
Hold on tight,
You're in for a ride,
Press against my body,
All pain petrified!

Words - words - beautiful words -
Flare out and surround us
Words - words - beautiful words -

It's the super natural
Ever bombastical
Little house of blur!
Scary and mirrored,
Exciting and dense.
Filled with adventure,
That will last till the end.
It's dark and it's twisted,
So hard to resist it.
Close up the space,
Enjoy all the bliss.

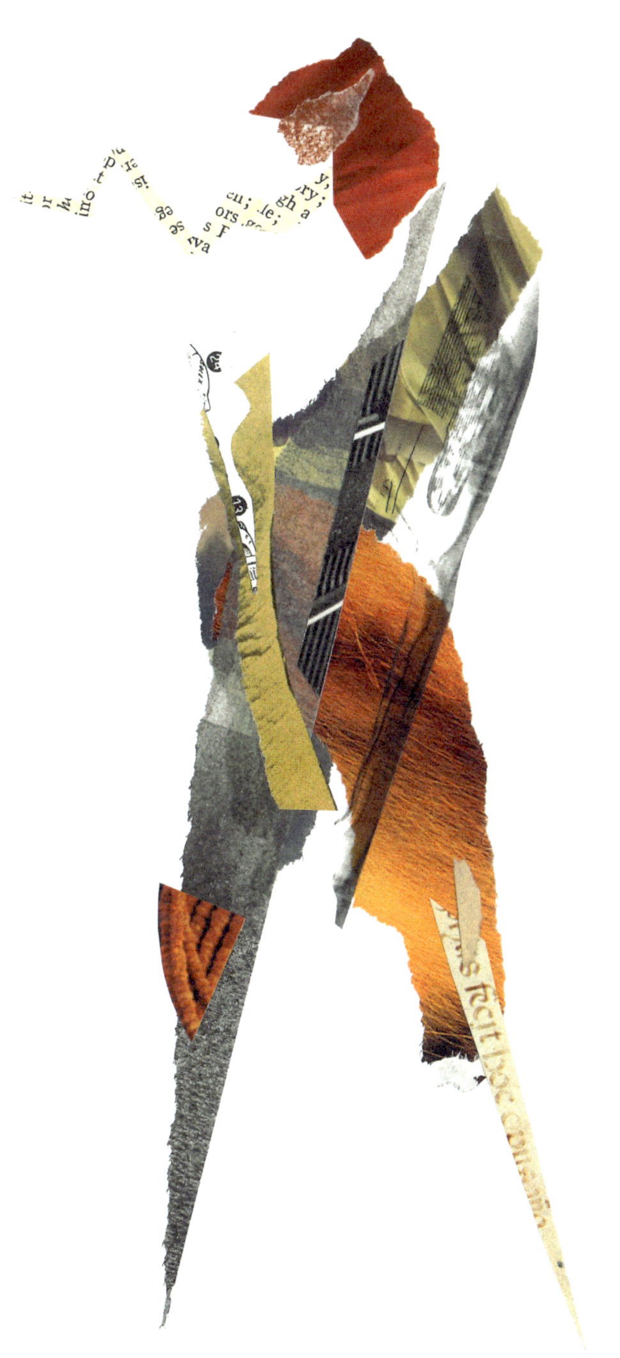

Weeping Wanderer

You wander through
- What you know to be -
Moments of forgotten glory.
Memories projected through
Blown sand.
Where is the hand
That you held so dearly?
It flickers in the peripheral
Of side space and closed hearts.
How did you capture melancholy?
Was it tossed on your being?
Or did you choose to leap off the edge
Into the arms of a saviour who jumped
Out of the way,
Leaving you to crash?

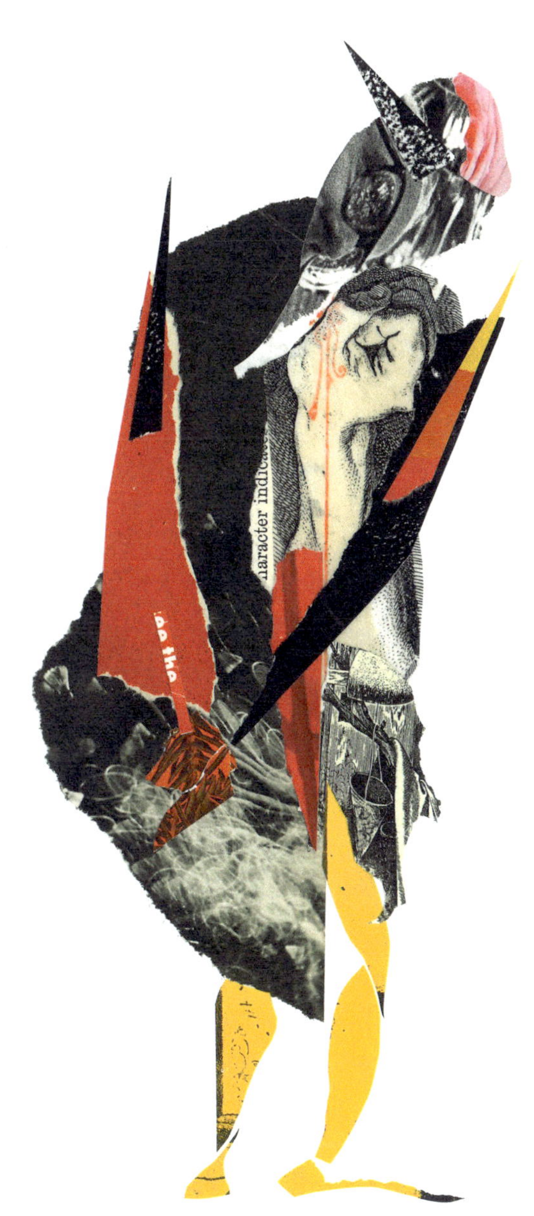

Cicada

Not unseen

She sits on leaves of gold
Surrounded by echos
Of things that hold
Once.
A warmth surrounds
The queen
She takes note
This is not tea time
- There is more -
Whispers of untold victories
Caress the air
It shivers with the tenseness
Of acknowledgment
- A secret nod -
Pressure in the third eye
Like a magician
- No -
More
A lapping of the ocean plays
Over and over
It captures the sound of rhythm
Cicada in the desert
Calm but intense.
Here comes the wave.
- I'm ready -

Is there order in the chaos?

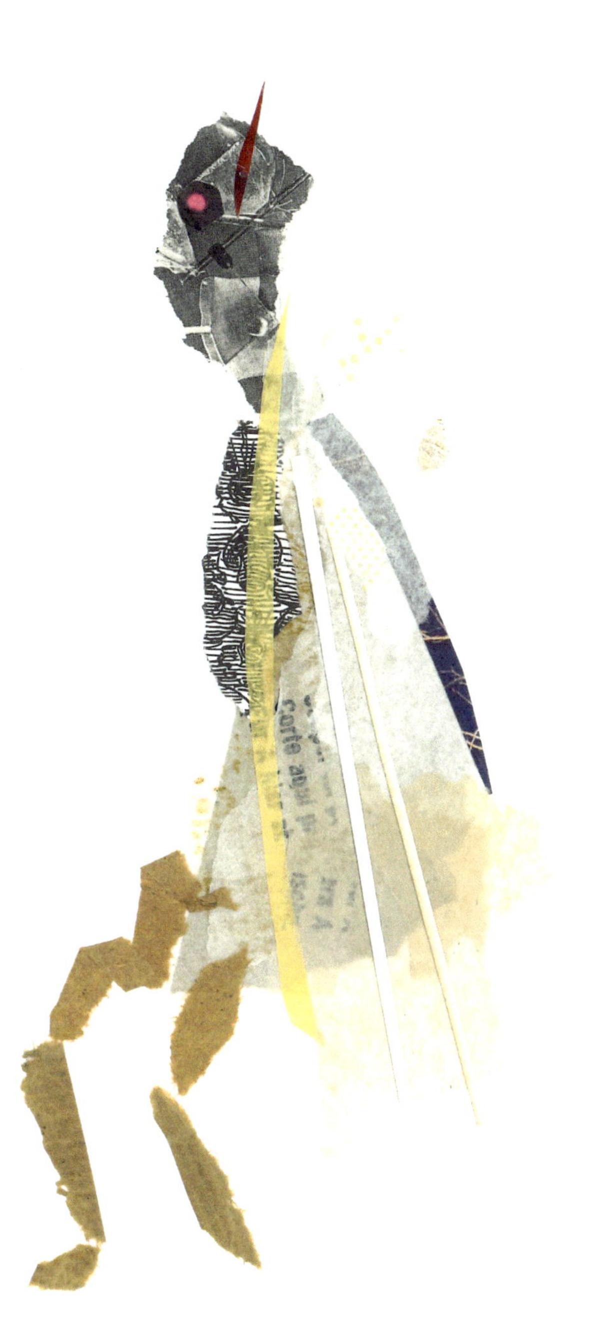

Fragment Breather

From intricacies of the unknown,
Worlds are built from fragment breaths.
Drops of swirled time touch hearts,
Most important is the start.

The stillness of a quiet lake,
Mountains go for miles and miles.
Silence in reverberations,
Full body and soul sensations.

Away from all the clash and clatter,
A stage is all that humans know.
Are there not wings in a production,
Shielding a calm world construction?

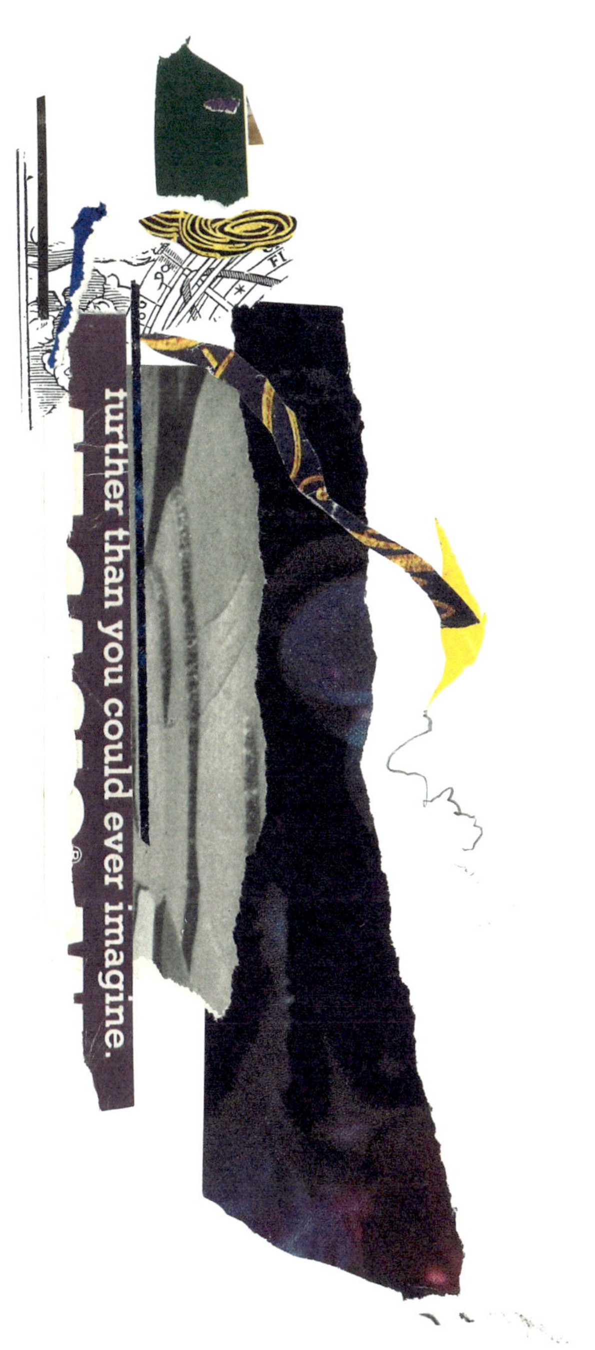
further than you could ever imagine.

Floaty One That Must Be Named

There is a space in the clouds,
That opens and closes,
Casting shadows and bringing light,
Shouting glory and bringing doubt.
From above or below,
The path changes its size,
When close to the sun,
It's easy to comprise,
That every moment is shadow free,
That the heart, mind, and soul,
Do not connect to the body.

- That fleshy container
It keeps one alive.
That fleshy container
It lets one survive. -

But imagine a moment
Where suspended in space,
That fleshy container is truly erased.
Would one still hover
Above the clouds?
Or float through poetry
And only be found -
In the beauty of being,
The moments of free,
A jellyfish existence
Made of eternity?

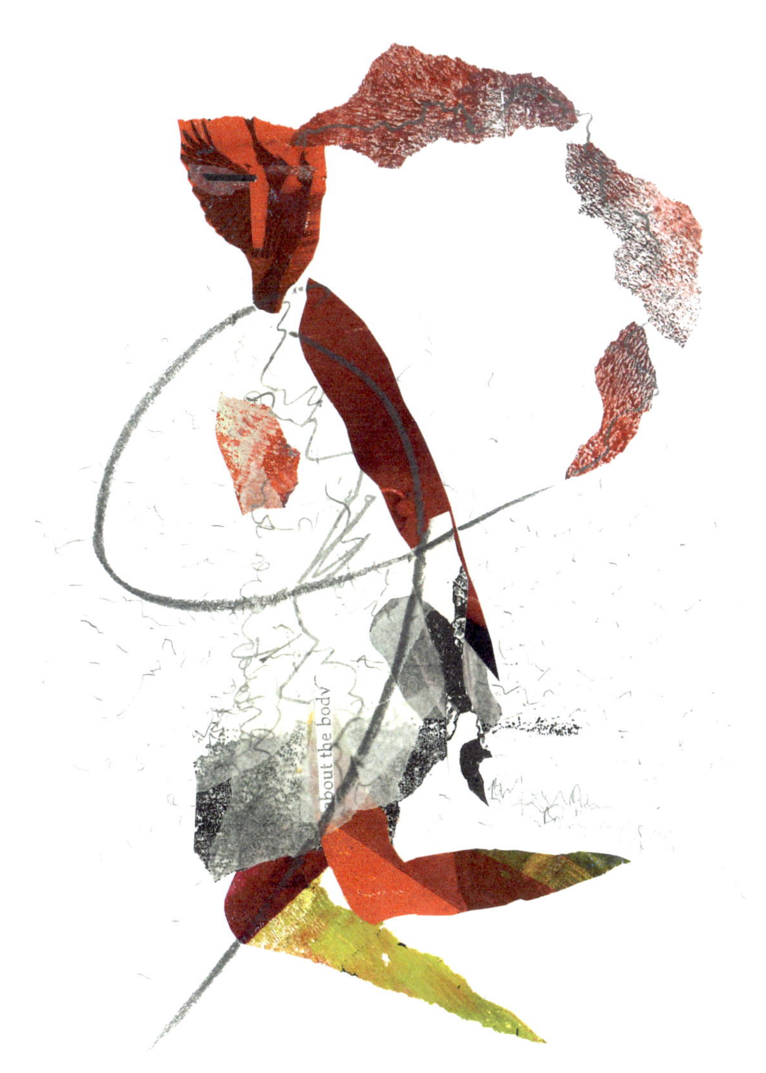
bout the bodv

Shadow Dancer

Naked
Naked
War
Naked naked war
Tears through her insides
Twisted fabric flowing dance
Through the air
Naked naked war
Naked
Naked
War

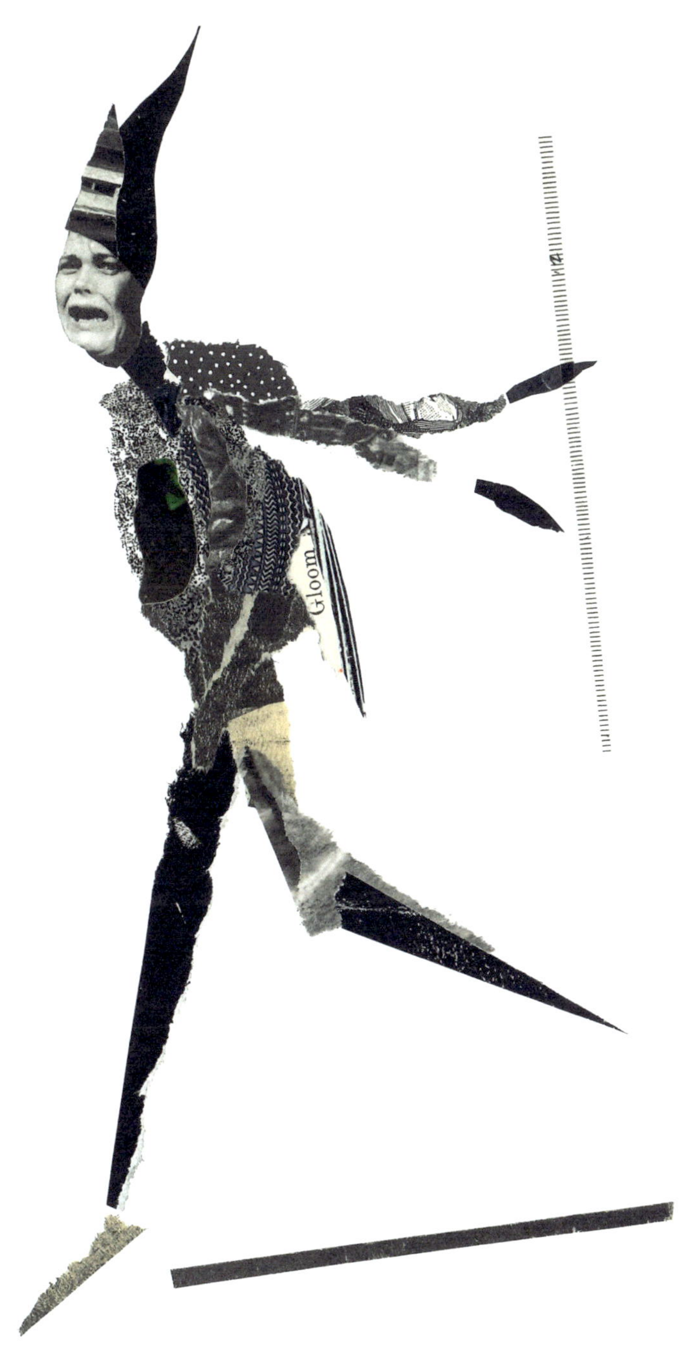
Gloom

Neuro-masseur

Beauty runs through me when I am with you,
A warmness that eliminates sorrow,
Bare danger of the lost and judged is true,
Sink in the water and glimpse tomorrow.

Bronze-hued ocean of incredible dark,
Progress that allows calm in moments blue,
Focus on innerness one must embark,
Sinking, grabbing all the light to pursue.

But if in a moment of carelessness,
Precautions are thrown high into the wind,
Dark aqua distorts true loves endlessness,
What brings pleasure will no longer be twinned.

Forever happy sorrow which brings truth,
Caution undone for perpetual youth.

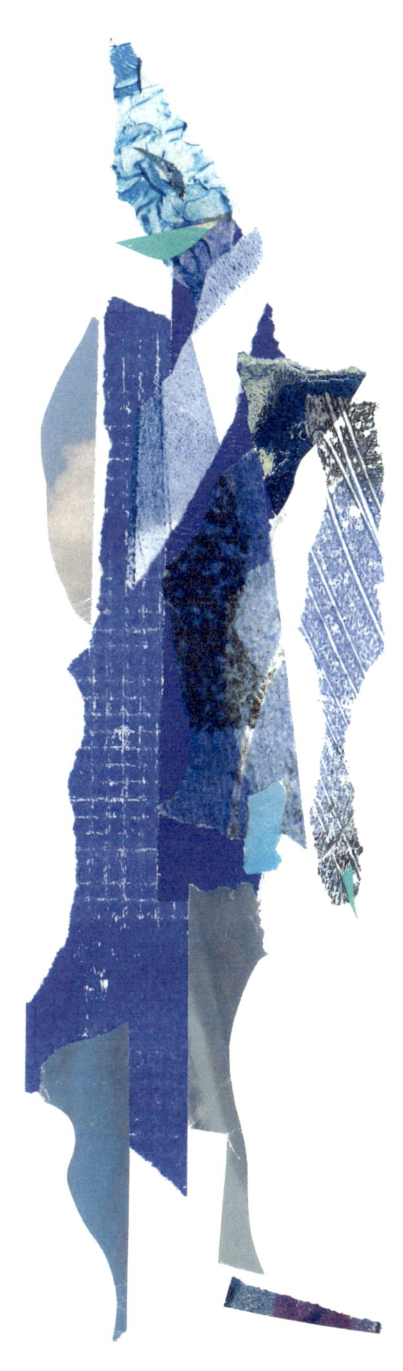

Sentry

All flowers start as wild,
They bind to no routine.
Happily they grow amongst,
Places never seen.

Until they are harvested,
Plucked out from a seed.
Twisted to new realities,
No more to be freed.

A sentry sits to guard them,
Nothing shall get past.
For in his silent aching,
He no longer is outcast.

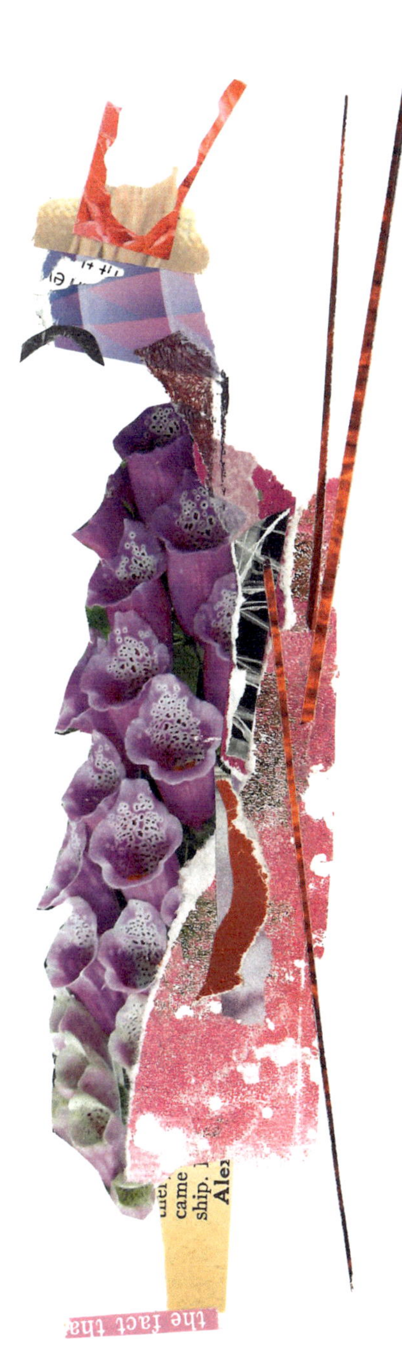

Swordsmith

I passed beneath your tattered frame,
I took without considering shame.
You placed me on a pedestal,
A guarantee of the longest fall.
With passions forged of shattered grain,
I gobbled them and filled my face,
And although the pieces did not aggregate,
They filled me well and calmed my fate.

I should have considered the price,
A pound of flesh it did entice.
You used a sword and took your desire,
Grabbing greedily you filled your fire.
Then you retreated and wrote a poem,
And wanted more,
You wanted home.
The silent pain that passion bore,
Should have stayed hidden in Shakespeare's lore.

What comes when the ashes fly,
Of attempted aggregates that die?
Nothing but an empty shell -
I reach out,
You repel.
What destiny lays in such a trial?
All just lessons of denial.

Come back to me my dearest friend,
Fill me with conversation that finds no end.
Wait in my mind with all your grace,
Take heed at a breakneck pace.
To forge a sword made out of steel,
An aggregate that you can wield.
And plunge it deeply in the soul,
For this alone will make you whole.

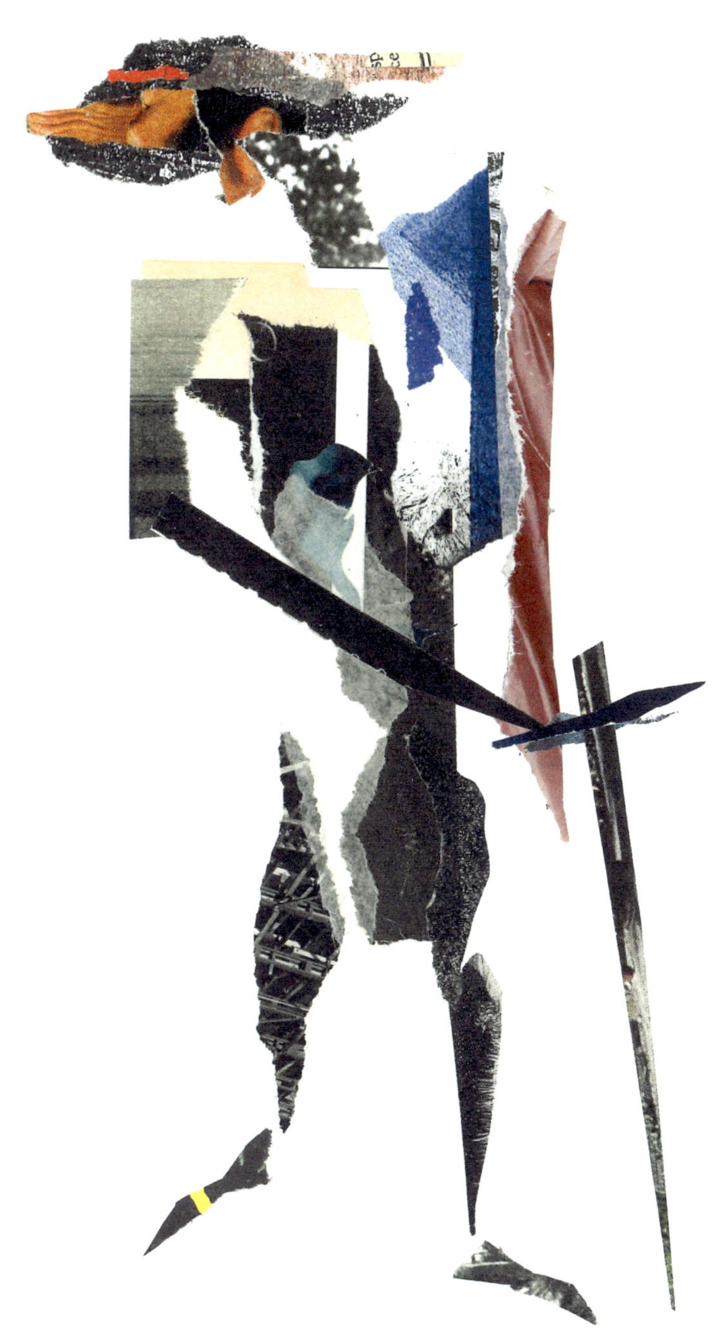

Underbelly

She claws the underbelly
Of this upside down reality
Gouging deeply into the fabric of its core.
Spiraling in nonsensical vibrations
Bellowing like a banshee into this said reality
Concluding a loud nevermore!
            This will never consume her -
            Assume her -
Fuck with her true reality
This fucking sad duality
The duality of insanity
That comes with a dirty evermore.

A false perception
Is a scared reflection
For those that slink along the ground.
They hold their breath in dying flesh
Choosing to consume what is fresh.
Feeding their false conception
Of their never ending obsession
With a very real perception -
            Of reality.
One not blinded by the crosses
Or the dogma of the masses.
Who hide behind a tongue of lies -
Their calculated choice to consume the eyes -
Of all victims that are willingly terrorized.
With a habit and a box -
A gobbling of the breath and soul
Salivated, swallowed and spit back out whole -

In the form of conformity.
Living in a false reality
This is a false reality!
Open your fucking eyes.

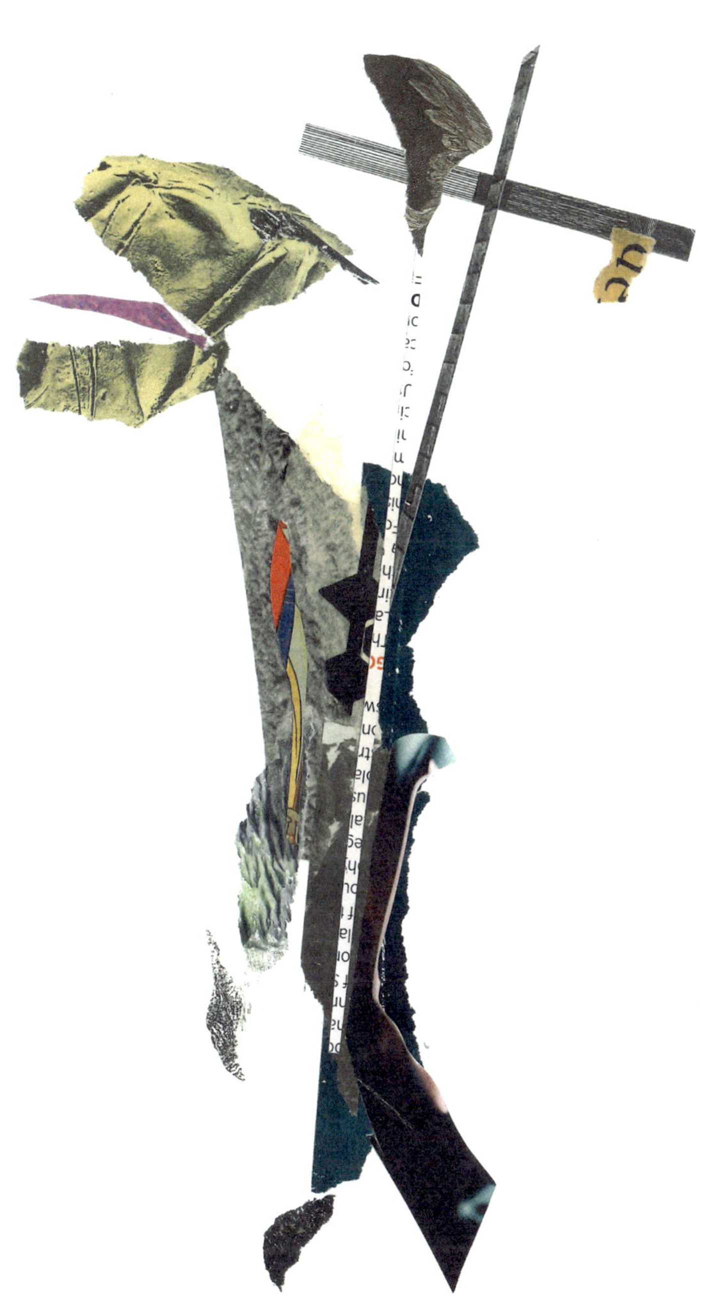

King Rat

Caught and captured in a trap,
Around and around goes the rat.
Gnawing at each spark of calm,
Trying to set off a giant bomb.

Wandering through the maze tonight,
Heart is racing - fight or flight?
Build a wall around my head,
Fight until that rat is dead.

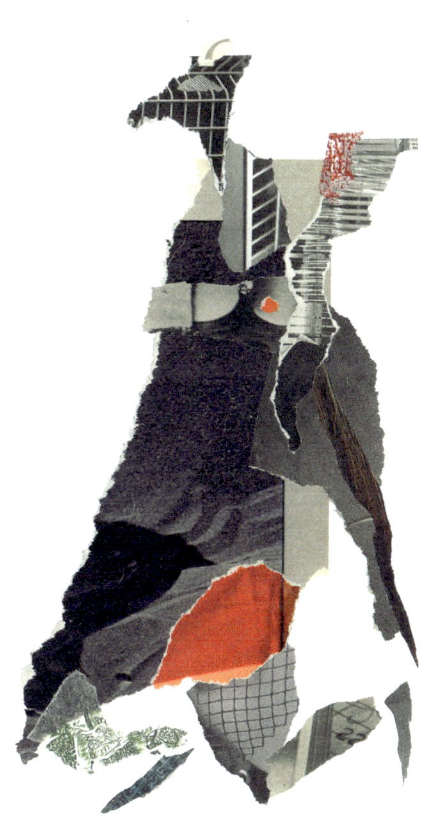

Sylph

Your head sits stooped in sadness,
Wings heavy in moth dust.
Time slants not only reason,
But the perfection of your touch.
You ate the rotten apple,
The one soaked in lost despair.
It pulled apart your insides,
With no care for how you'd fair.

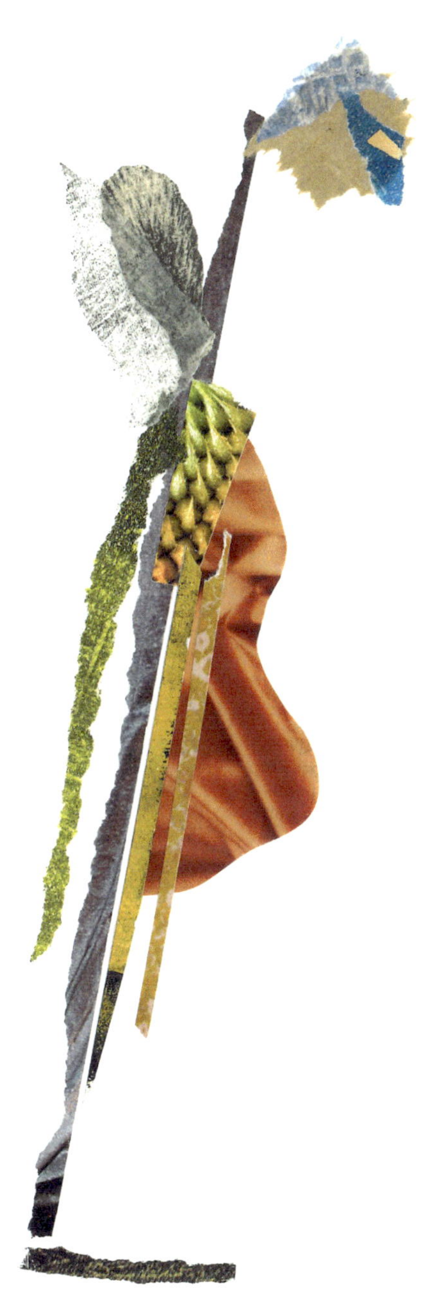

Guide

To the depths of the catacombs,
We shall go!
When fortune ventured upon insult,
An obsessive thirst did grow.
Those deeds that hide behind smiling eyes,
Villainous malice,
Twinkles of earthly demise.
How be you, Sir?
How be you, Ma'am?
Twinkle twinkle
A bird captured in hand,
Looking down the corridors grande.
Go back if you must,
You probably should.
No? Then follow,
Damp stone and sharp wood.
Bells jingle from a conical cap,
Sniffing out solace,
Through a desire to tap.
Built upon a pile of bones,
Stone upon stone,
The wall starts to enclose.
Against the new masonry,
A screaming silence ensues.
Walking alone from the catacombs,
Deep thirst now defused.

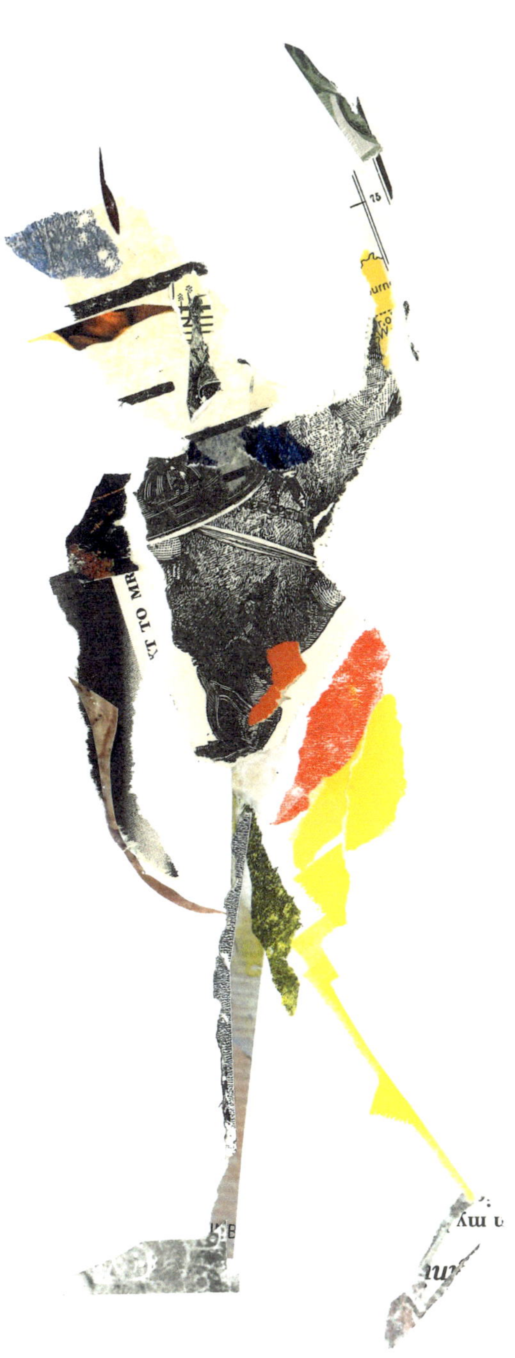

Prancer

I saw the sky fall when I died,
It laughed and pranced at me -
With a silent whisper of eternal,
I knew it would always be -

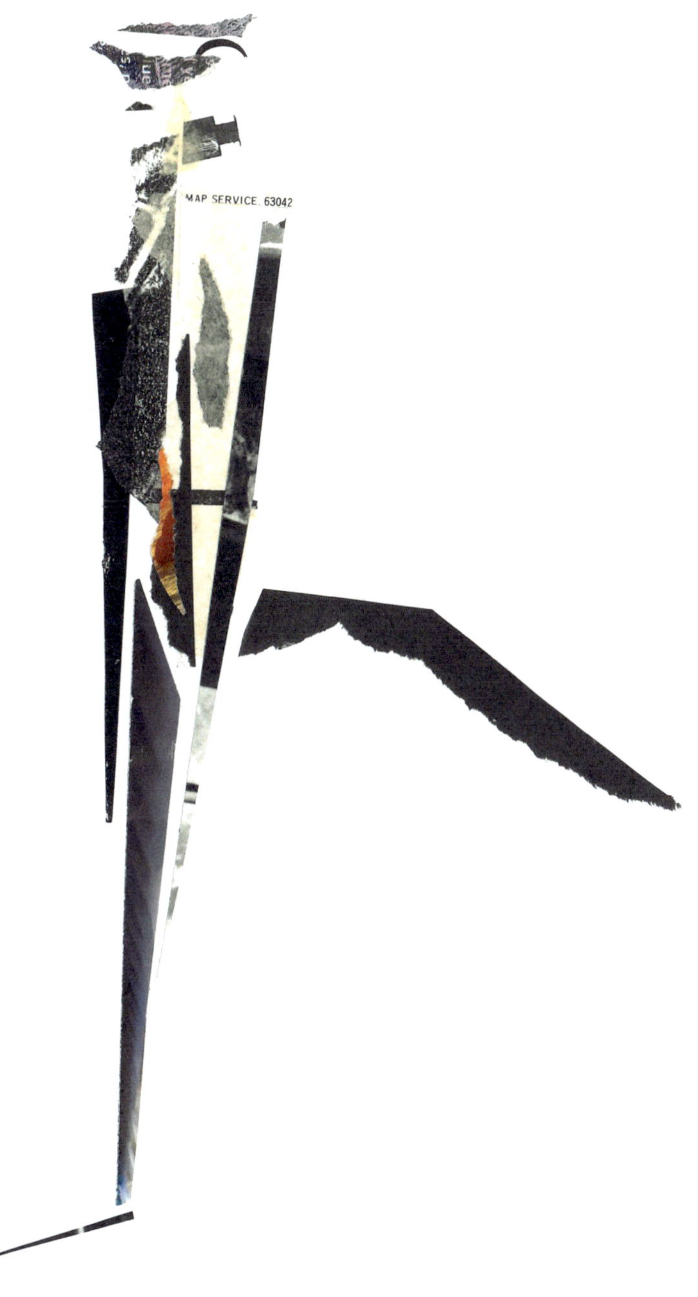
MAP SERVICE. 63042

Lenore

A raven came from the unknown,
Perched within a dream.
A peace that surrounded it,
Silenced all the scream.

Horror swirled around us,
In this dreadful hopeless theme.
Yet the raven perched beside me,
Paying no attention to the scene.

Upon the waking hour,
(I shiver to repeat)
A poem came from the universe,
Delivering the oubliette.

The trap door now was open,
With sun streams shining in.
Bathing in the sunlight,
I chose to stop the spin.

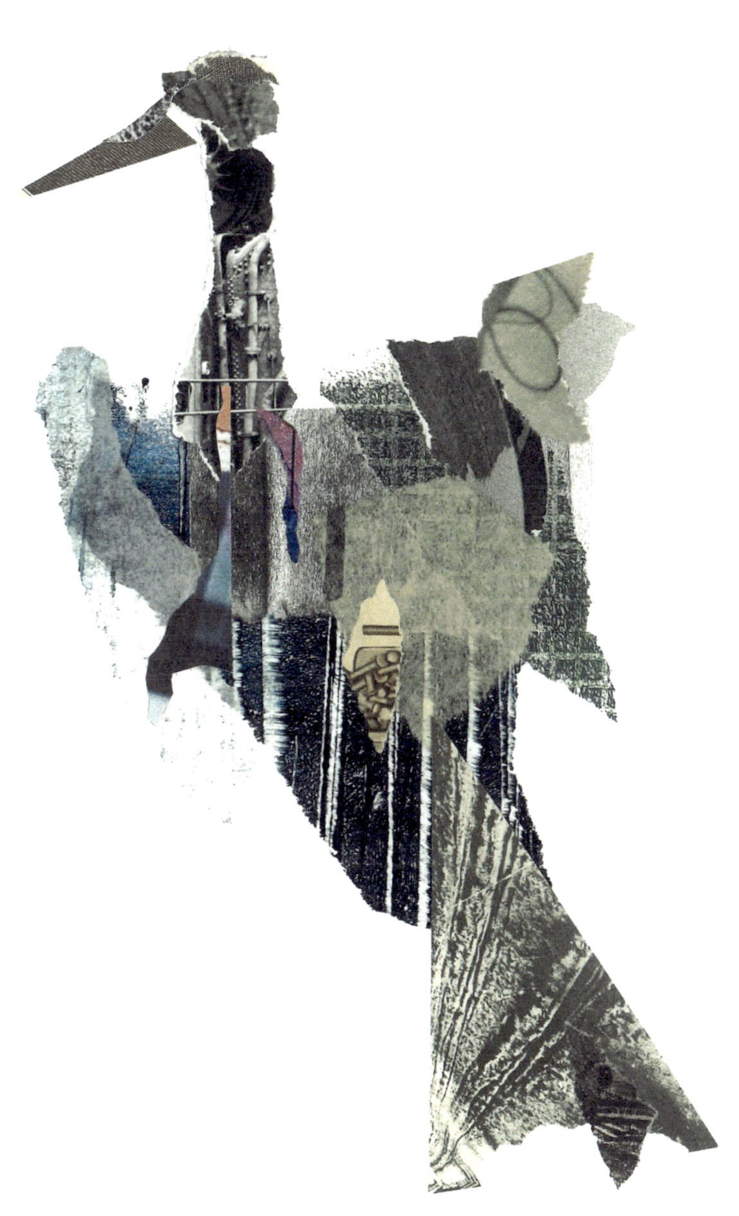

Incrementalist

Always moving forward
Never looking back
A continent of knowledge
Colliding right on track.
Features of chaotic calm
Solo fireflies of song
Listen! Listen!
It's all wrong,

- Breath still -

Sultry caresses
Of a head held high
Whisper successes
That rapidly intensify.
Moulded in charismatic charm
Fully filled all along
Feel! Feel!
There's nothing wrong,

- Hold fast -

Jumbled arms
Of knowing sighs
Feeling harms
Without the tries.
Pasted to perfection's lore
Following what's in store
Look! Look!
It's tumbling down,

- Just be -

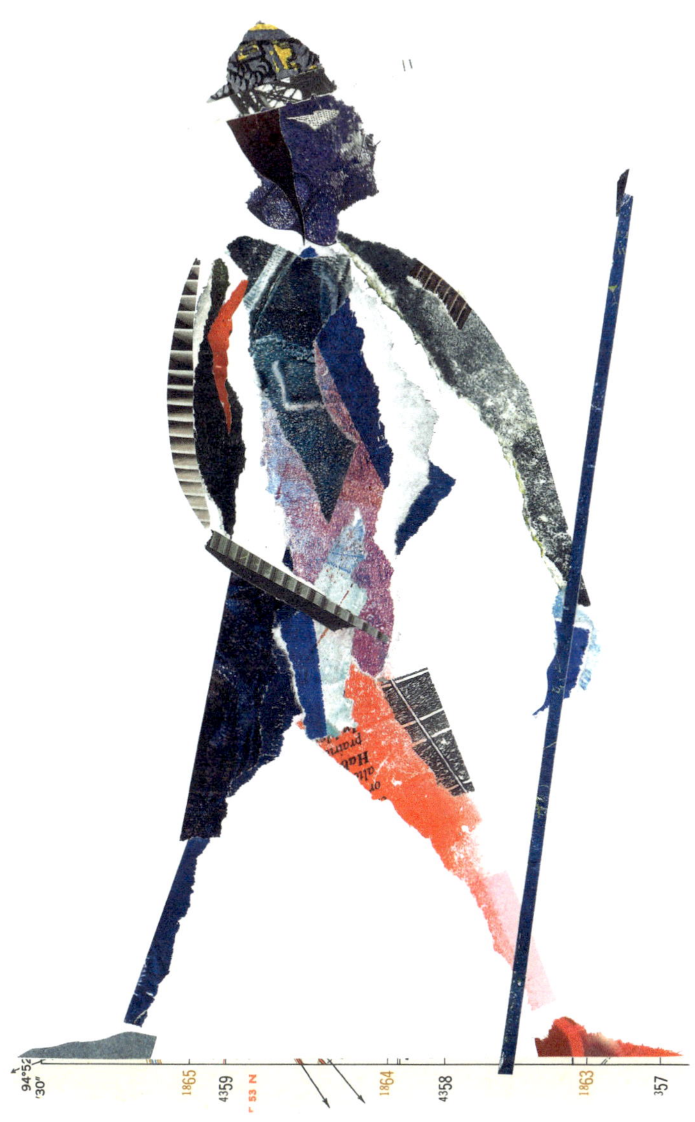

Ephemeral Soul

The lake of longing,
Holds the key.
Sparkling wishes,
And magical trees.
Calling from the blue unknown,
A distorted body,
With an ephemeral soul.
Come I tell you!
Come with me!
Leap and listen,
What will it be?
Shall we capture unseen time?
Dance like dervishes,
In a toppled mind?
Or throw a wish into the air,
Sliding ravenously with zero care?

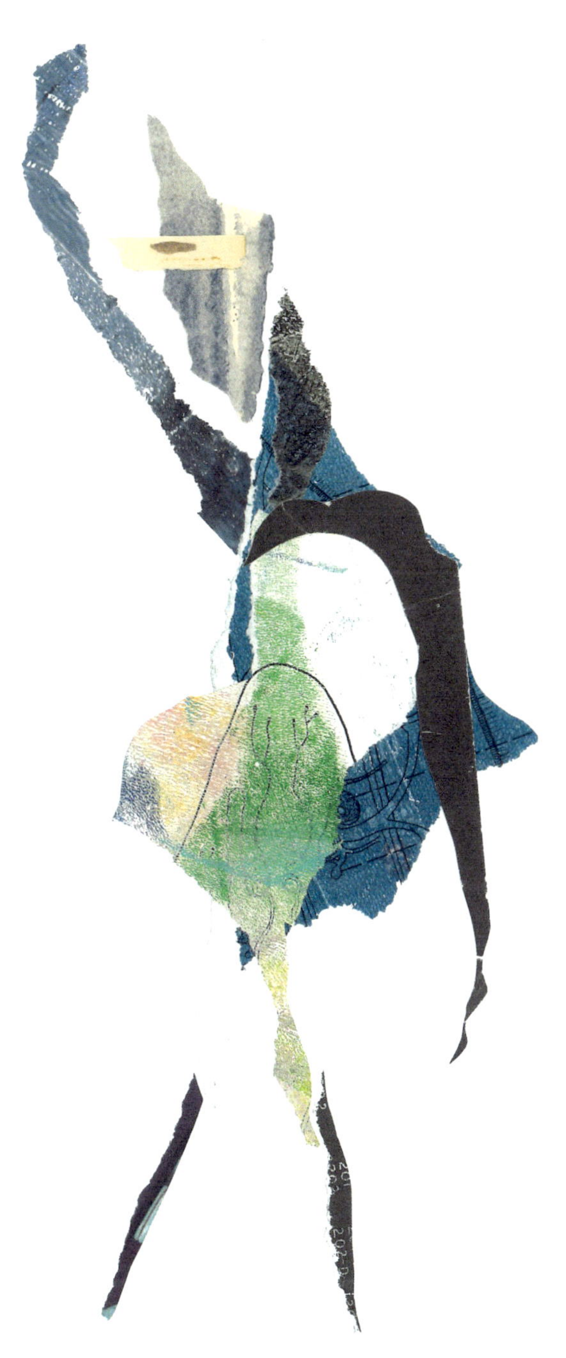

Thinker

My heart drops
With each missed thought
As I venture into the blue.

A maze at night
Hides the plight
Of everything meant to be true.

The brain spiral
Holds a trial
Of sights unseen or heard.

They sit in the lost land
Whispering that singular word.

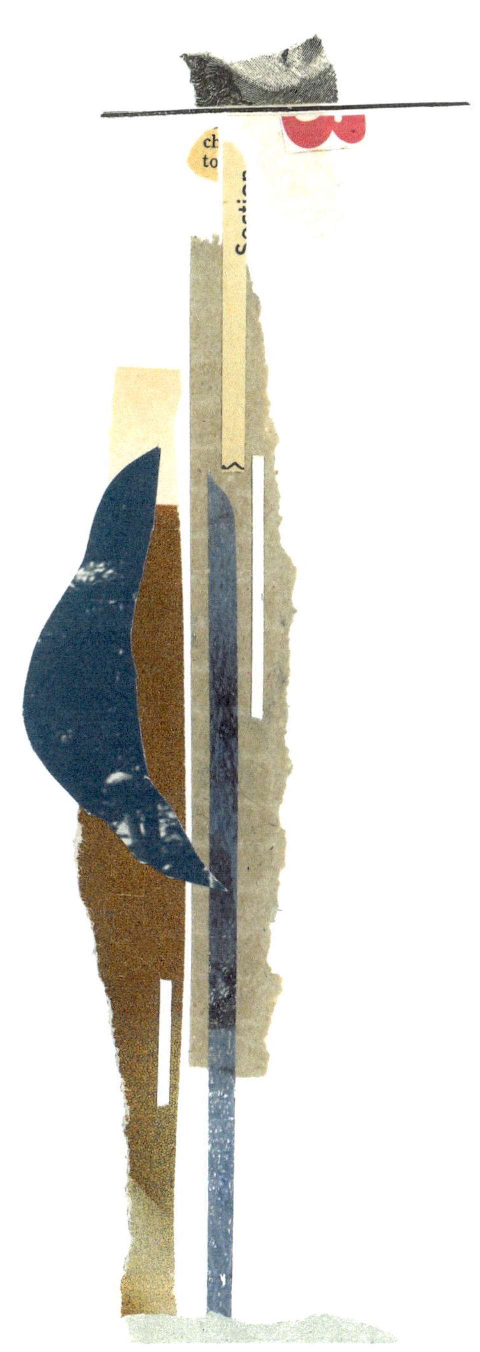

Caged Bird

A bird in a cage will only stay
Because it is held captive.
The sky is free to sail and be
Why won't you go and fly there?
Something's clipping your wings,
Stopping the song to sing.

- Each day you grow weaker -

Look out to the sky,
Say your goodbye.
Move through the window
You made there.

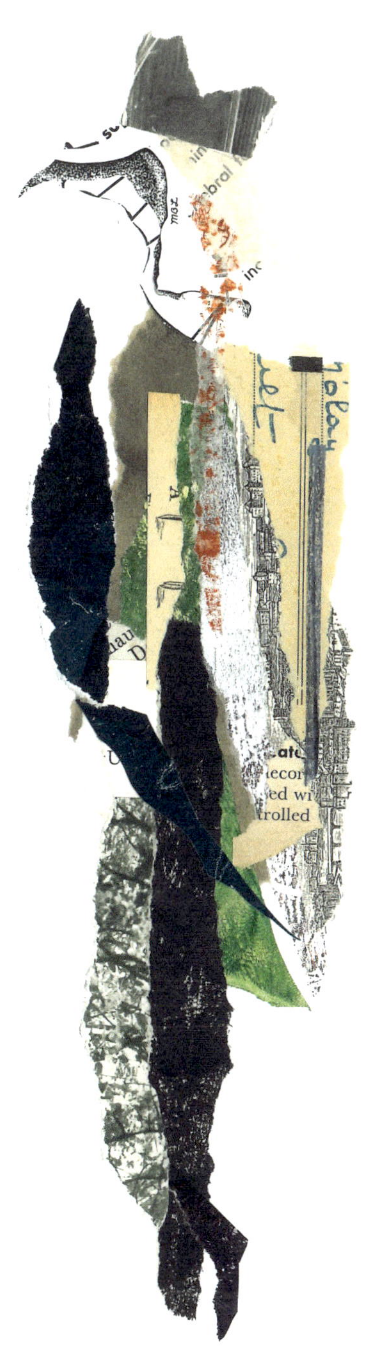

Pneuma

Flickering to the moonlight,
Twisting embers all around.
Fingers stretch in broken greens,
Colours rarely found.

Pillar of destruction,
Creating a haven full of life.
Ephemeral breathing,
In a garden of earthly delight.

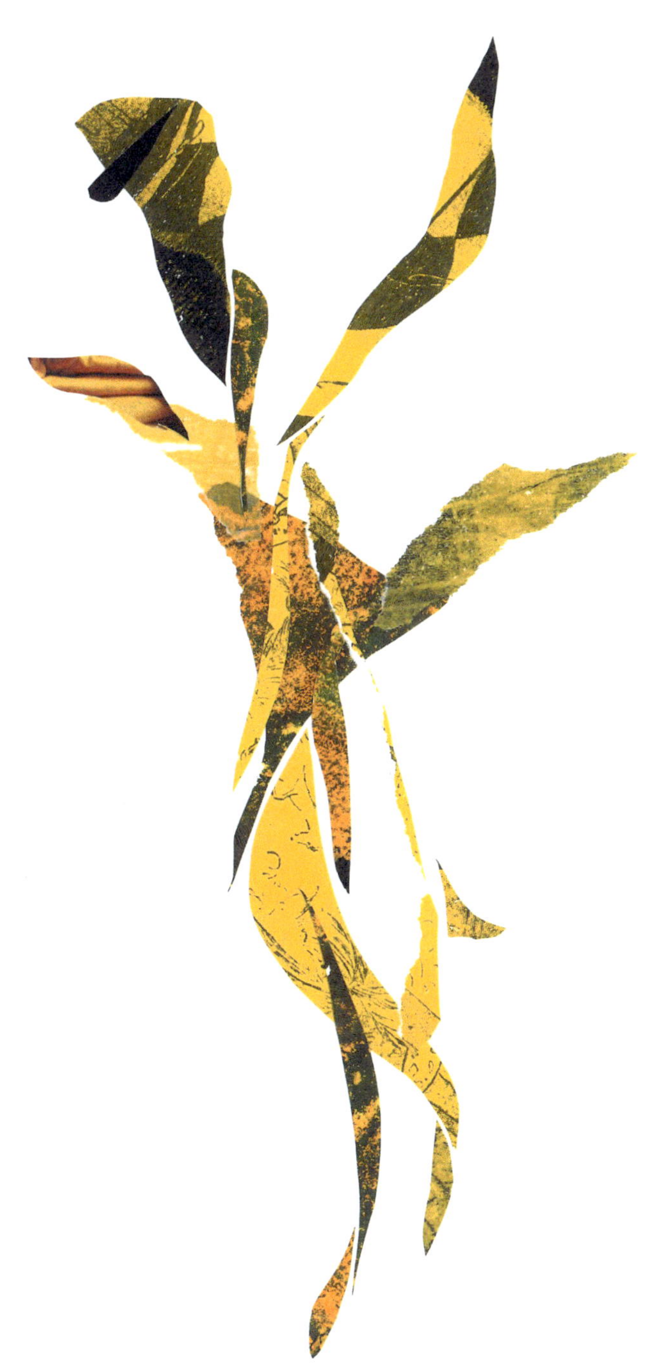

Moon Thief

In reference to the heart,
It's not on hold.
There are battles fought,
Stories to be told.
Eternity is carried in the eyes,
A still, sad, sense of humanity's
Unwillingness to compromise.

There are moments,
That are written in the sand.
Washed away by waves,
Held in your hand.
Spirals swirl constantly inside,
Commanding confusion,
Forcing another tide.

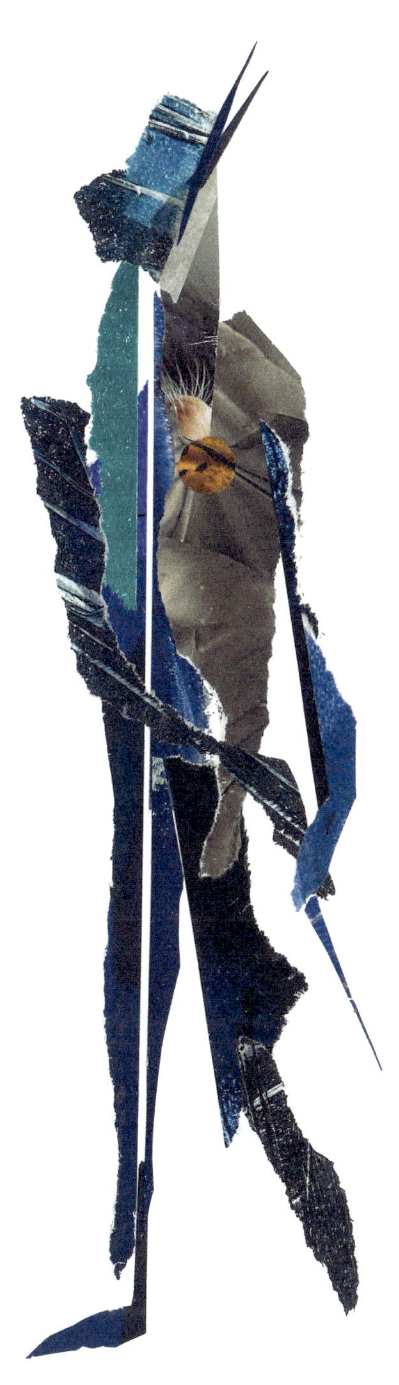

Vagrant

I see the sadness that covers eyes,
I see those who have compromised,
Slinking in their demeanour,
From being pushed down -
From being gobbled and spit out -
And stomped while on the ground -
They rose like phoenixes each and every time.

- Except that last time -

They stayed a pile of broken,
Fragments, and specks of ash.

- Ah, one spark! -

That was quickly dashed.

And there are fields
Of ash piles -
They go for miles and miles.
And around them walk the new -
Upright with a spark that blazes blue.
And they see the piles but pay no note,
Because the piles get higher and the ground just grows.
Then there are those that see it all,
That try to sweep away the mounds.
They know because they were the mounds -
Their spark was fostered by forces known,
An "in", some golf, a tonal shift.
How about him? How about this?
They are groomed to be the next makers of mounds.
They are just happy to own the grounds -
The land of ash and mounds is theirs!

Like a wraith I hover there.

We are the ones that are not mounds -
We are the ones that do not own the grounds -
We saw the flame and saw it damped -
We saw it continuously stamped -
The Phoenix broken from within,
Its wings held out and finally thinned.

- We float freely above the masses
To stay around and yell silently
So the owners know they are not free -

As much as they would like to think -
It's in their swallow, with every drink.
Poison, "a woman's weapon" -
Metaphorically is knowledge protection.

Knowledge of all that has been done,
Chokes the owners continuously -
It holds their throat and bends the knees.
But of course... only privately -
It's a system built of fear,
In the world I see it clear,
I roam amongst the tainted world -
And stand and swirl and swirl and swirl.

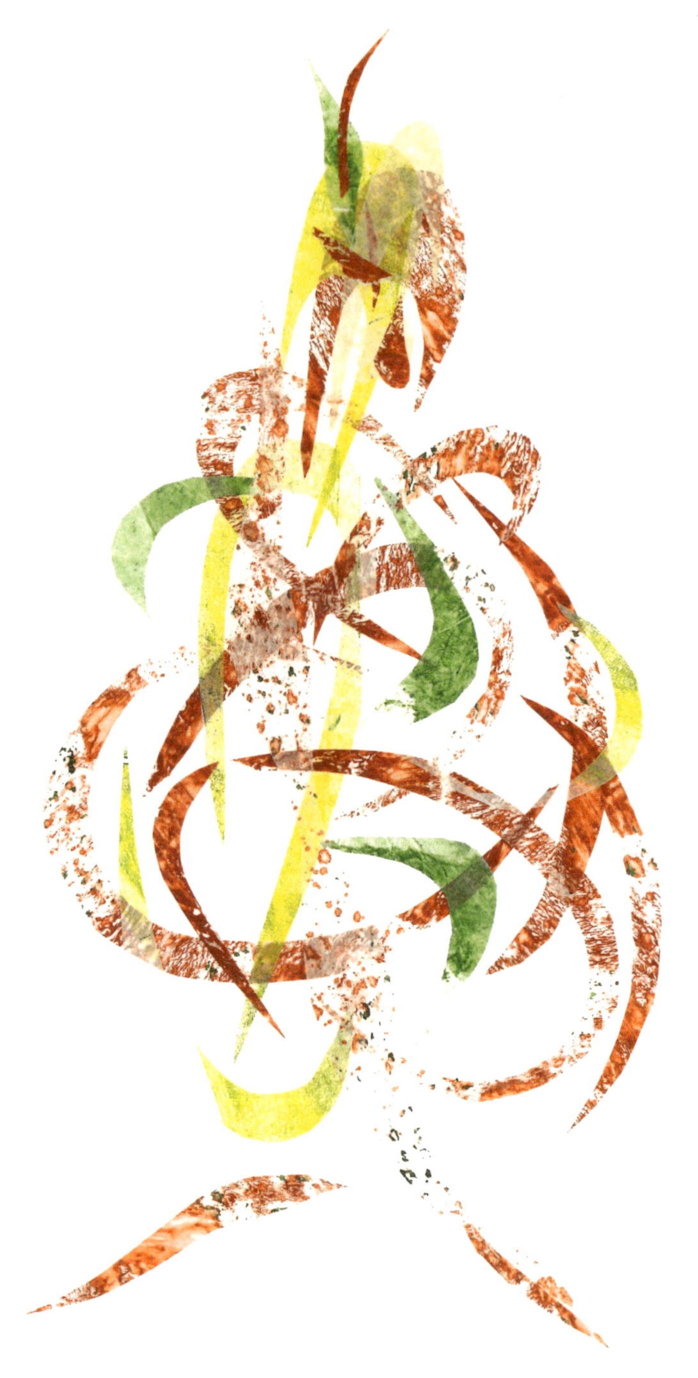

About the Creators

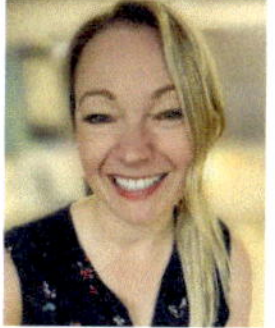

Terriann Walling is a poet and High School English teacher in Saskatoon, Saskatchewan, Canada. She holds an honors degree in English, a Bachelor's degree in Education, and a Master's Degree in English from the University of Saskatchewan. Her main area of study was Twentieth-Century American Literature and Literary Trauma Theory. She is a published poet and artist with local and worldwide collaborative works. She co-hosts a podcast called 'Speak it Slant' which can be found on Spotify and YouTube. She loves her family and believes that time is a construct and that fairies exist. Her most recent book of poems is currently available, titled *Forest Dweller*.

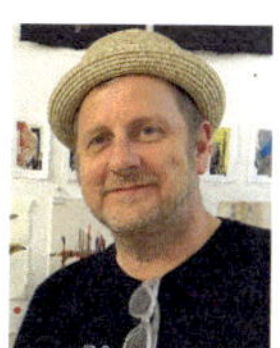

Clive Knights is an English collagist, printmaker and professor of architecture in Portland, Oregon, USA. Alongside professional degrees in architectural design he holds a Master of Philosophy from Cambridge University. His career as a teacher has been inspired by the phenomenology of the human body and the hermeneutics of gesture. He has published widely on architectural theory and pedagogy, and has exhibited his collage and printmaking work in over forty group shows and five solo shows in the USA and several European countries. His most recent book of collages is currently available, titled *Gestures from a Body at Work: Unsuccessful Attempts at Grasping Eternity.*

Made in the USA
Columbia, SC
12 October 2024

43473029R00069